HORSES:

From Our Side of the Fence

Sandy Lagno

First Printing November 2007

ISBN: 978-0-9788394-1-3

Printed in the United States of America

Published by:

Beneficence

Power Spirit Freedom Movement

A spirit-centered business for consciousness.

Gratitude to all that come forth to present their full potential.

Supporting all those standing in their gifts.

Allowing the freedom to move in spirit on this earth.

Your power... Your spirit...

Your freedom... Your movement!

www.beneficence.net
Cheryl Rennels
970-222-5184
cheryl@beneficence.net
Box 99, Livermore, CO 80536

Publishing • Private Consulting

Books • Products • Classes • Outreach

For People • For Animals

be·nef·i·cence (bə-nef′ə-sens), *n.* actively doing good.

In memory of Ed Lagno, my dad, and Obviously A Sonny, "Sunny," my last horse. I am grateful to both of them for the doors they opened.

To Betty Lagno, my mom. Thanks for believing in me when I didn't.

Credits

Publisher:	Beneficence, Inc. Cheryl Rennels www.beneficence.net
Editor:	Ann Streett-Joslin www.RanchoVistaLLC.com
Cover Design:	David Santillanes DigiGraphics, Fort Collins, Colorado
Cover Photo:	Judy Barnes www.JudyBarnesPhotography.com
Reading:	Carol Spiciarich Mahoney Mahoney Consulting, LLC Fort Collins, Colorado

Acknowledgments

My sincere gratitude goes to all who were involved with this project. Your help and support made this book a reality.

Cheryl Rennels, my publisher - Thanks for taking a chance on the horses and me.

Ann Streett-Joslin, my editor - Thanks for listening!!

Cindy Reich, my first supporter - Thank you for the Monday meetings that kept me writing.

Patty Lagno, my sister - Special thanks for tough love when I needed it.

Susan Beal, DVM - Thanks for the many hours of listening on the phone.

Sarah Smith - Thanks for allowing your horses to be photographed for the front cover.

My heartfelt thanks to Sri Gary Olsen for the MasterPath teachings.

And thanks to all my clients for your wonderful support.

Sandy Lagno

There is only one horse on the earth
and his name is All Horses.

Carl Sandberg

Contents

The Beginning

Dominion - Fall 1991

"Come on Dominion! Stand still. Then we can both go to bed!"

It is ten o'clock, Friday night. Opening Meet, the most formal and traditional event of the fox hunting season, is at eight o'clock tomorrow morning. Horses and riders are expected to be turned out perfectly. For the horse, this means mane and tail braided, coat groomed to white-glove perfection and tack gleaming. For the rider, boots highly polished, stock tie and clothes spotlessly clean and hunt cap sitting squarely. Getting ready is a production.

"Dominion, does 'no carrots for a month' mean anything to you? Not one tiny carrot? A whole month?"

Dominion, an 11 year-old, 17 hand, Warmblood gelding, is standing cross-tied in the wash stall. I am on a step stool trying to braid the mane on his very long neck, which means *lots* of braids. I hate braiding and get extremely cranky, even on a good day. Having to braid a horse that is shaking his neck and fidgeting around makes me want to scream. But I do not resort to physical punishment with horses, even when they don't stand still.

"What is it? What do you want? Please stand still and this will go much faster, promise."

You have heard the adage, "be careful what you ask for." Dominion turns his elegant head toward me as far as the cross-ties allow. Inside my head I hear, *"Take my halter off."*

The braid slips out of my fingers, and you could knock me off the step stool with a feather. There are no mind-altering substances in my system, past or present, that I can blame for this moment. I retort, "Yeah, right! Take your halter off and you'll run out the barn door, and I'll spend the rest of the night looking for you. No way, bucko!"

He lets out a sigh and goes back to fidgeting. I go back to pleading and threatening no carrots for a year. I put him in his stall to see if he has to pee. Nope.

"Do you want to look like a D-1 Pony Clubber braided you? Where's your self respect?" *More shaking and stomping.*

"We'll be looked at in disgrace!" *Fidget, shift.*

"Do you want the Master of Foxhounds to dismiss us from the field?" Pause, head turns and looks my way. *"Take my halter OFF!"*

You could hear a pin drop in the barn. Even the other horses are quiet in their stalls. Nothing stirs. I look at Dominion and think, "Can this be real? Did I really hear him say, 'Take my halter off?' Am I hearing horses?"

I have worked so hard to be normal. I do not want people to think, "Oh, that crazy Sandy Lagno. She's a sweet lady, but the elevator doesn't go to the top floor." Please, God, no!

"Dominion, suck it up. I hate this as much as you do, so get over it!" *Wiggle, squirm.*

"Does the word 'Alpo' mean anything to you?" *Shake cross-tie chains, shift feet.*

"Does the word 'knacker' mean anything to you?" He pauses and looks right at me for the third time. *"TAKE MY HALTER OFF!"*

There is no doubt this time—what I hear in my head is absolutely crystal clear. Dominion really is asking me to take off his halter! This goes against my Pony Club training, many years working professionally teaching horse safety and all the years with my mentor, Deborah Dows, who had training at the Spanish Riding School. Do I trust years of learning from expert horsemen or *myself*? Nothing has prepared me for this moment.

By closing the bottom half of the barn Dutch door, the worst that can happen is Dominion will walk out of the wash stall and go to his own stall. No big deal.

"Ok, you win. I'll take your halter off."

I close the bottom half of the door and unhook the cross-tie chains, letting them drop. Then, I unbuckle Dominion's halter and let it slide off. He presses the front of his face into my chest and sighs softly. I step back onto the stool. Dominion drops his head and stands as still as a horse statue. We finish braiding peacefully. It is so simple.

I know something special has happened between Dominion and me. I do not understand it and certainly do not tell anyone for fear of the ridicule that would come my way. Who will believe me? I wouldn't believe the story myself!

Fear of looking bad, sounding crazy or being judged stupid is a powerful force. I am here and even doubt it myself. In my heart, I know "hearing" Dominion in my head is real, but my mind says I made it up.

A New Door Opens - 1993-1997

In January of 1993, my right knee was shattered in a pasture accident, ending my ability to ride professionally. Prior to the accident, I could put a solid base on young horses that would become field hunters. My teaching specialty was starting young children and timid or fearful adults to ride.

I didn't achieve my dream of riding at the upper levels, so I saw myself as a failure. I did not see then that I had the skill and understanding it takes to successfully start young horses and riders. I know now that seeing myself as a failure all these years is the cause of my self-doubt.

After the accident, the physical challenge was huge, but the emotional one was much harder. Riding was my life's passion. The loss was shattering. It took a year of rehab and another year of hard work to regain the use of my right leg. I was finally able to walk without a limp.

With that accident, a door had closed in my life, but in April 1995, another was thrown wide open for me. I attended an animal communication workshop in Canada because a friend called and said, "You need to do this." Within the first hour, I knew I could "hear" animals, especially horses. It had been four years since that night with Dominion, and I now knew and accepted that I could hear horses. For the rest of the workshop, I was consciously aware of the gift I had possessed all along. Figuring out what to do about it was a major leap of faith.

For the next two years, the horses kept after me. "You can hear us! We want you to tell our stories to other humans." It became harder and harder to ignore them. Finally in 1997, with the horses pushing me hard, I shouted, "Enough! I'll do it, just stop badgering me!" So I started letting people know I could communicate with animals, and the translation work began. It was my "coming out" year.

Charismatic - June 1999

The next milestone occurred when the Thoroughbred Horse of the Year, Charismatic, broke his leg racing in June of 1999. I did not make enough from translation work to make ends meet, so I was cleaning houses with my friend Lori. The day after Charismatic broke his leg, Lori and I were cleaning a rental house. I was in the kitchen scrubbing a dirty stove when I "heard" Charismatic in my head. His message was very strong; it was clear he had things he needed to show me. I tried to show him I was low-ranking in the human herd, and maybe he needed to communicate with a more important human. Charismatic was very definite it was *me* he had things to show! He knew I could hear him—period. I was compelled to stop cleaning, get my notebook and start writing what he showed me.

Lori walked into the kitchen and saw me writing. She was angry I was not cleaning—we were on a tight schedule that day. I explained to her that Charismatic was showing me what he wanted humans to know about breaking his leg, and that it was important to him. Lori looked at me, shook her head and said, "We have to get this house done." I did not move and quietly said, "Lori, I have to do this." She replied, "Why now?" I said, "It's just the way it is. When information comes, I have to listen and write." It was a tense moment. Lori walked out of the room and I continued to write.

I was beginning to trust I was really hearing horses, yet it was still a struggle. The question I kept asking was, "Why me?" The horses replied, "Why not you? You hear us clearly." To them, it was that simple. I thought only "important" people got to do this stuff. The horses saw me differently. To them, *I* was important. It was difficult trusting that this should come to me, even though my whole life had been with horses. The horses told me to trust.

The following is what Charismatic showed me that day. As I wrote, Charismatic felt peaceful and respected. I felt his great strength of spirit.

Breaking my leg - no accident. No accidents. Humans need - see - result use our bodies - before our bodies grown.

I chose this - blessed - support. I am calm. I no fear. My jockey knows. My jockey honorable human. He felt my spirit - we race. He ignores connection - connection there. He knows more of horses than - way is. He - I - fly. I ran - choice run. Others of my kin - run of fear. Humans close of me - know I special.

I came as teacher. Show humans - error - way is done now. Humans know stress of us - no change rules. Rules racing - need change. We ask - of humans.

Honor us.

We give much - some us - our lives - to humans. We willing - work of humans. Why humans - no work us - compassionately? We magnificent. We run - humans watch - thrill.

We give gift. Power we are - so are humans. Thrill - humans feel - reminder - to humans.

Humans more - than humans think.

I ask - my humans - search hearts - in sorrow of me. I no blame - my jockey. No anger.

I ask - see - door open. New way - using of us. We want - continue run. We ask - run as older bodies. No babies. We ask - treatment of us - respect. Humans - see us - as things. We flesh - spirit - as humans are.

We ask - no racing stop - healthier way doing of us.

We give much - of humans. Open humans heart - see needs done.

Humans know - in hearts - injustices - humans heads rule. Humans heads - see - power substance.

Humans hearts - see - beauty - grace - courage. We are such. Humans hearts recognize - humans mind no listen.

I ask humans - see hearts. Changes made benefit us - benefit humans. Racing evolve - higher level. We honored - honoring us - humans honor humans.

Discomfort need no happened.

Humans sorrow of me. Search humans hearts. Many humans - see - change happen.

Beauty of us flying - true thrill of heart. Hollow one now.

Humans - love of me - guide humans.

Look past discomfort - look solutions.

I honor humans - know this. My jockey knows. He felt me - no other has. We bond.

Speak for me - for others. Please.

Thank you for trusting - hearing through you. Trust this.

I sat at the kitchen table in amazement. When I went back to cleaning, I knew something very special had happened. Now that I had Charismatic's message, I thought, "What do I do with it?"

After a day of wondering what to do, I contacted the Jockey Club and found I could send mail to Charismatic's owners and jockey through them. I wrote a cover letter, enclosed a copy of what Charismatic showed me and mailed it to them. I don't know if they received it; I did not hear back. I had not expected to.

Mailing off Charismatic's message was a stretch for me, but it was impossible to ignore the strength of that message or to let it stop with me. Charismatic wanted his owners and jockey to know how racing was for him and the other horses. He was telling humans that they race horses too young. His body broke down from the physical stress on bones not fully formed. We know this, but for economic reasons, continue to race horses young anyway. I sent the letters for Charismatic.

Horses are willing to race—some of them love to race. The thrill we get when we watch a group of horses pounding down the track is okay with horses. They provide this thrill for us graciously and willingly. Charismatic is asking that healthy changes be made to support horses in their job of racing. He is asking us to work with horses in a mutually respectful way and to see horses as beings of spirit, like us, rather than things.

In the summer of 2006, Barbaro broke his leg racing in the Preakness. Charismatic's message again came to mind. It is still important, seven years later, maybe more so now. How many more horses will break legs before we will pay attention to what the horses are asking of us?

New Mexico - June 2000

In the summer of 2000, I was working with a group of horses in New Mexico. These horses showed me they wanted me to tell humans their stories and point of view. I thought about it for a minute, and I saw that a book would be a great way of getting horses' stories to a larger group of humans. The horses didn't know what a book was, but they got excited when *I* saw a way to tell other humans their stories. The earnest way they looked at me sent a chill down my spine. They made it clear this was important to them. Horses wanted humans to know what it is like for them to be with humans. I was speechless.

True to being me, I immediately balked. "Why me?" My excuses went like this:

> "I barely passed English to graduate from high school."
>
> "What do I know about writing a book? Nothing."
>
> "I am not well known in the communication world. Who will take me seriously?"
>
> "All that new writers get from publishers is rejection. I've had enough rejection!"
>
> "If I write this book and if I get it published, my private, quiet life might not be so quiet and private anymore. This really scares me. I like my cave."

I told the horses, "Isn't it enough I do the work I do?" "Nope," came their reply. The horses wanted bigger coverage—they wanted me to tell their stories. Horses, being the persistent bunch they are, kept the pressure on for four more years, the same way they did between 1995 and 1997.

Leap of Faith - June 2004

I'm one of God's slower learners. Apparently, since 1997 I had not learned from all my experiences with horses like Charismatic, that I am capable of doing more than I think I can. You've heard, "What you resist persists." I did all the same things as I did with Charismatic—"not important human," etc. Always the response was, "You hear us clearly." It was so simple to them. Why did I, as a human, make it so hard? Childhood conditioning? The old, "my parents didn't love me enough," routine? No, that one doesn't wash; my parents were great.

I was a horse-crazy child. We lived on Staten Island, New York, and my Dad bought me a horse when I was five. Then we moved to a farm ninety miles north of the city so I could have my horse, Gypsy, at home. Dad gave me a great start and Mom, even though horses frightened her, let me follow my passion. It was a real challenge for her.

Horses were a huge influence in my growing up. When I was upset about something, I always ran to the barn for comfort. Now here I am, years later, being pushed to write a book. How could I refuse these wonderful horses who had given me so much all my life? So in June of 2004, at the insistence of the horses, I agreed to write their book.

The Agreement

My agreement with the horses, as individuals and as a collective, is to translate, uncut, what they "show" me. I translate what they show me as accurately as possible and let it stand on its own. The horses have made it clear that if I edit, interpret or otherwise tamper with what they show me, they will no longer show me anything. This is not an easy line to walk, and the horses are not easy taskmasters.

The ground rule is that I work only with the horses' permission. I go where they lead me and translate their information on the topics they select. The chapters are presented in the horse's order, not a logical human order. They contain what horses want humans to know about their topics. With permission from the horses, I have added clarifications to assist the reader. I have to keep reminding myself, this is *their* book. I need to stay out of my ego and stop thinking I know better.

So this *is* the horses' book. I simply translate. The horses, as a collective, want humans to know how *they* view their world and what it is like to interact with humans. This is not another feel-good view of horses. This book simply gives the horses' point of view about their lives and how it is for them to fit into a world of human rules. Their message is unedited. There is no judgment or expectation on the part of the horses to change the industry or to change any individual's mind about how they see horses.

The Translation

I work telepathically with animals. Information flows in both directions in a mind-to-mind connection. Horses do not communicate in words. They communicate in a mixture of pictures, sounds and emotions—what I call "whole thought forms." This telepathic exchange happens so quickly in my head that it seems as if I hear in words. The night with Dominion is an example. When I said that I heard him say to take his halter off, I did not really "hear," and he did not really "say." His information came in a flash. Horses use telepathy all the time.

I take all this information—the pictures, sounds and emotions—and translate it into words. It is similar to translating a foreign language. I connect directly with the horses, as they are often trying to connect with their humans. From the horses' point of view, most humans do not use their telepathic ability.

I am only able to go where a horse takes me and receive what that horse wants to show me. There may be five things the human asks about, while the horse may show me only one. If a headache is what concerns the horse most, then that is what I am shown. Eventually, by my working back and forth between the horse and human, I am able to bring both the horse's and human's points of view to the table. It is not a straight line.

"Point of view" is important for both sides. Telepathy is two-way and is truly the heart of inter-species communication. I have the ability to show horses pictures when I need to make something clear to them. In a respectful way, I work to help the horse understand the human's point of view. I may offer other options the horse may not have known were available and then ask for cooperation. The horse can choose to cooperate or not. Also, I help the human to understand their horse's point of view. My work is about clarity for both sides. With clarity comes understanding. In understanding, solutions are available.

The Message

Throughout this book, the words "show" and "shown" are used extensively. This is what horses do when they give their point of view. As the context requires, I have occasionally substituted words such as explain, reveal, say, share, speak, tell, told, etc. Please keep in mind that the input from the horses is in a collage of pictures, sounds and emotions.

For the rest of this book, in an effort to help the reader, the text is broken into two columns when the horses are speaking. The left column is the horse's information. The right column contains my explanations of words or ideas that humans might not necessarily understand. For example, in the chapter on training, horses see a "training session" as an "explaining gathering."

Here are some points that I feel are important when reading this book:

- My translation work is not a replacement for clear, consistent training.
- Anthropomorphism plays no part here. I do not place human characteristics or human emotions on horses. Horses do have emotions on their level, but not on the human level. They are not the same.
- Horses live in the moment, however they do have memories. Their memories, both positive and negative, influence their actions and reactions.
- When I translate, I do not try to become part of the horse herd. Humans often try to act like a dominant horse, but horses know we are two different species. They are prey animals and we are predators. I am not trying to become a "horse" in order to translate.
- Even though mental telepathy is a psychic phenomenon, my work is very specific. I work directly with the horses' minds and can see only what the horses allow me to receive.

- Horses do not communicate all the time as humans do. A telepathic link is not permanently established between the horses and me. I do not have the right to intrude. I must ask for permission to work. Animals only communicate when they have something to show me. The rest of the time they are quiet.

Since the chapters are presented in the horses' order, the book, as a whole, does not flow chronologically. The information within each chapter is chronological and has the ability to stand on its own. As each chapter unfolds, I share my experiences of the events happening in my life as I worked with the horses.

I did not choose the traditional publishing route. A door opened, and a publisher and editor were presented to me who were horsewomen and very respectful of horses. They pushed me hard for good composition and correct grammar. Well, the horses and I don't work that way. At one point, everything was "correct," but the book was so flat it had no life. The horses turned their butts to me, effectively giving me the cold fanny. Horses don't know about language. What they do know is flow, movement and how things feel. So, the grammar and composition are loose, and in some places, I did override recommendations from my publisher and my editor.

Allow yourself to get caught up in the movement of the pictures in the words. The horses' text has a raw power and beauty of its own. The essence of their message flows through the words with movement and rhythm. It is like poetry in a syntax that may seem a bit foreign at first.

The horses' messages are presented without judgment or expectation. The horses simply ask us to consider their point of view. They have raised many issues that exist in the horse industry today. Horses are horses with horse behavior; our current practices in housing and handling horses are far removed from their wild, herd environment.

As readers, I invite you to consider what the horses have said. The horses are sharing their point of view with humans as a gift. They want humans to have a deeper awareness of the horses' world. They are teaching me that with greater awareness comes the ability to see many solutions to issues and problems.

The horses took me on a journey to write this book, forever changing my life. Please read it from your heart, because it is given to us from the heart of these generous beings. Now I turn you over to them.

The Horses

Chapter 1

Stallions & Breeding

A stallion's job is the two P's: protection and procreation. A stallion patrols the perimeter of his band, always on the alert, to defend his mares from other stallions and predators.

Competing, challenging and fighting with other stallions are all part of a stallion's nature. They fight until one gives up or is dead. Young stallions in a "bachelor band" spar to build the skills needed to start their own band. In the process, a hierarchy is built that keeps order in the bachelor bands. The smartest, strongest and toughest not only earn the respect of the bachelors, but eventually, the respect of a lead mare.

Now enter humans. We have created a stallion environment to suit *us.* This means breed only when asked, and be gentlemen the rest of the time. It also means keeping individual stallions separated from each other and from mares. This is contrary to their social nature.

In this chapter, I have translated what different stallions had to say about being in an environment created by humans. As I sat next to their pens or stalls, it was amazing to have the collection of pictures, sounds and emotions come into my head. At times, it was difficult to stay objective. Here is what the stallions showed me.

Capitol

Thoroughbred stallion. Brown, no markings. 17 hands.

Capitol was one of the most handsome stallions I had ever seen. He was a former racing stallion with perfect conformation, a "ten." For six months I helped care for him and felt privileged to walk him from his stall to the outside pen each day. Not everyone was allowed to handle him, as he could be a handful. Capitol was not nasty. He knew he was big and sometimes used his size, especially with smaller humans like me. We had an agreement—he would walk like a gentleman, and I would trust him to do just that. Our arrangement worked well, and he liked that I could hear him. I miss seeing him every day.

June 10, 2004

Capitol asked me to sit by his pen as he had things to show me about how it was to be a stallion.

Being stallion - big job.

We wild herds our job stallion clearer. We lived pace all we contact with - water - land - sky - all live in those domains.

We lived rhythm seasons where birth - death - simple part - rhythm.

Birth and death are part of the simple rhythm of all life.

Breeding time governed by seasons rhythm. Stallion earned respect his band mares. Breeding came - mares dictate - no our whim.

Our job stallion - protect - procreate. Mares - conceive - nurture - run herd.

Herd numbers reflect food available - plentiful - lean. Lean years kept us strong. Humans panic lean. We flow rhythm lean. Some us died lean season - simply was. Death part rhythm of us. Holding no fear of us.

My cells hold memories wild existence of us.

I live human created environment of stallion. Our contact of humans - with our agreement. Our contact mutual benefit both sides. From our side we give generously - use our large bodies. We easily overpower humans anytime we choose. Mostly we choose cooperate.

June 11, 2004

I was again sitting by his pen listening. Capitol had more to show me.

Stallion - human environment I confined. Covered confinement - under sky confinement. Humans dictate where I confined relation sun position. Non-sun position I covered place. I no non-sun sky over me. No starlight light my body. No non-sun air movement touch me.

covered confinement = stall

under sky confinement = pen or paddock

non-sun = night

Under sky place - falling water - I brought covered place. Falling water good feeling my body. Humans curious mental patterns doing life.

falling water = rain

I see other stallions. No touch of them. Only physical contact another horse breeding mare.

To be registered, Thoroughbreds must be bred by live cover. Artificial insemination (AI) is not allowed.

All movement - human dictated. I walk beside human covered place to under sky place. My movement controlled - straps on my head - metal snake over my nose - leather snake attached - human holding. I move too much human pulls metal snake - distracting me - walk slow.

metal snake = chain shank

leather snake = lead

As Capitol showed me this, I felt sad in my heart for him and his confined life. He felt this from me, and he moved closer to the fence, looking directly into my eyes. This was his response…

Little human, no see my life sadly. I anytime no do humans ask me. My place - I accept. Other stallions lives harder of mine. Lead mare human looks well of me. My place - no accidents.	My place is here. He is reminding me that each of us chooses where to be. lead mare human = barn manager
I remember running - I miss running. I choose relax now. Unhappy - waste energy. Other stallions unhappy - I smarter. I very smart. Know live suit me.	He accepts his life.

June 16, 2004

Sitting by Capitol's pen.

I miss running. Best - race days. I knew race days - air tingle. My touch human extra particular - me ready. I miss touch human - gentle hands. Touch human sang me - calming me. Touch human - voice soft. Touch human heart - show me run on wings. Of all humans his image stays me.	touch human = groom
Humans think we no run. Horse running best job. Our bodies made run away predators. We run - young of our bodies.	Some humans think horses should not race. The trouble is racing too young.
Sun - sharp discomfort - came my left front leg. Stress - bone no fully formed. My touch human crying heart of me.	The day he sustained a fracture while racing.
I taken big smelly place. Humans run smelly place repair. I walk. My job running ended. I new roofed place. My touch human gone. New touch human of me. My leg hurt - I confused. Humans did	big smelly place = veterinary clinic

things of me. No human explained happen of me. Things done of me. I angry.	He did not understand what was happening to him.
Humans no ask horses we want.	Humans don't ask permission.
Humans assume role. I moved place I now live - no human thought about me - I wanted go place. We have memories - we no dwell. We live now - moment. We see humans thoughts. Humans thoughts smudged - jumble. Few humans clear thoughts. Clear thoughts humans - easy of us work.	
My job - breeding stallion. I breed mare. My physical contact of horse. I see horses. No touch them.	Breeding is his only horse contact. He can see other stallions and mares but can't touch them.
Physical union of mare/me holds vital spark creation. Moment vital spark - humans miss truth of.	The vital spark is stronger in a live cover and less vital in an AI breeding.
Breeding manipulated - of humans. No act - consent in herd. Movement diminished - no of actual breeding. Miss freedom - consent. Movement - our choice.	
Humans pick mares - we no choose. Humans no always - pick strong mares. We choose strong mares - embody wholeness.	wholeness = health
Create strong foals - strong partners required. Why humans miss - mystery of us.	
Vital spark critical - create strong foal. Breaking down our bodies - human based - through humans - breed us - feed us - handle us - harsh liquids us - environment we live in - how much movement allowed? All factors simple of us - left our own choices. We know in our being - to do. Humans use minds - no always accurate.	harsh liquids = drugs, vaccines, chemicals Human management affects the horse's vital spark.

July 6, 2004

Sitting by Capitol's pen.

Stallions problem breeding - humans assume we behaving badly. Remedy - sharp reprimand - show force - assuming force fix problem - bringing us job now.

Humans think force will fix problems and make stallions do their job immediately.

No occur humans look further bad behavior. Rarely humans ask us we feel. We encourage humans - remember ability hearing of us.

Humans rarely look beyond bad behavior for a cause.

ability hearing us = telepathy

Reasons us trouble breeding. Discomfort - frustration - no like mare - bad handling - poor feed - anger - loss confidence - tired - confusion - no enough exercise.

Big hindrance of us - human attitude of us. Humans see job we do - breed. Humans forget we horses - horse behavior. Beings - own right. Have feelings. Thoughts our own. We expected perform mechanical way. Humans lined us many mares of us. Humans thoughts power - concept foreign of us. Of us humans demand our bodies - breed.

lined us = booked many mares

power = money

Is no we saying we no want do breeding. We ask humans work with us - awake conscious way of us. We ask humans - consider carefully before breeding us - following:

Ask humans to work with them in a more aware/conscious state regarding breeding.

1. Why humans want create foal?

2. What happens foal?

3. What job foal do when mature?

4. Present numbers horses total: Surplus? Shortage? If surplus why create more foals?

5. How stallion chosen? What criteria? How move? Stamina? Intelligence? Special job? Importance human standings? Willingness? What expectation of us? Well formed body?

special job = e.g. racing, reining, jumping

importance human standings = earnings, ribbons

6. How mare chosen? What criteria? Good leader? Sound? Temperament? Well formed body? Good nurturer? Mare want foal? Special job? Stamina? Intelligence? Good discipliner of foal?

We no asking system. We asking humans - be aware humans doing. Ask above questions. Humans find answers - affect humans choose do.

They do not want regimentation. The answers to the questions will affect what humans do.

We ask humans - consider these things. Considering these things change perspective - possible. Considering these things - humans partner of us more wholly. Stress calmer both sides. Changes open creating balance - now unbalance.

We no expecting change quickly. Aware awake conscious state change possible. We maintain willingness - honor agreement made suns - moons - seasons cycles long passing.

Horses have no concept of time.
sun = day
moon = month
seasons cycles = year

We ask respect - our being.

July 8, 2004

Sitting by Capitol's pen.

We show separation stallions this sun.

Hard of us - separated other horses. We endure treatment - best our nature. Touch we receive of humans helps. Poor replacement. Touch another horse - our nature.

Way horses touch each other - in humans seeing - rough. Our biting - kicking - we horses. We break skin - raise bump - we no concerned. We no concerned we look. We aware our bodies placed together. Scars symbol our worthiness of breeding. Humans us no scars.

A picture of an unblemished, perfectly formed stallion, which they see in our minds.

bodies placed together = conformation

We no understand humans wanting our bodies untouched. We perfect we are. Contact - interaction between us - importance of us. We prove ourselves right of breeding. We spar - non-serious encounter. Right of breeding encounter - serious intent. Sparring encounter builds skills of fight - stops short serious injury - death.

A picture of a stallion with scars and bumps on his body.

Interactions important - development wholeness. We experience release tension - like release seed breeding. Helps us rhythm life. Interaction different intensities - different stages our lives.

interactions = fighting or sparring

Images of young, middle age, and old stallions.

We miss contact. We live humans dictate - remain obedient of humans. Stallions frustrated - humans label us bad. We ask humans see - cause our frustration - no use more force - no tighter confinement as remedy - humans use of us. We ask humans - see - feel our frustration - make changes we managed - handled.

We feel humans response - fear of us. Humans fear our powerful bodies. Humans fear we damaged of our bodies. Perpetuates present system management.

Humans have rigid thoughts around how stallions, especially very valuable ones, should be managed because they fear the stallions will get hurt.

Humans belief - humans know best of us. Stallions breed mares. Humans well intended. Humans well intention - keeps us honoring agreement.

Humans choose which stallions breed which mares.

We ask humans consider humans treat - manage us - our point view in humans mind.

Ask humans to consider their point of view.

We no blame humans. System developed suns - moons - seasons cycles long passing. Change possible - benefit us. No smooth easy be humans thought - mind way. We work with humans. We ask humans - open humans self of us - hear us. Mare human hearing me - hears inside.

mare human = author

Campy

Warmblood stallion.

Campy was a very valuable stallion trained in jumping and dressage with a large booking for the breeding season. He had a sweet disposition, was well-mannered, very much a gentleman and a delight to be around. He developed a problem where he could no longer release semen when breeding.

July 8, 2004

I was asked to see if there was anything Campy could show me that would help the veterinarian working on his case. A couple of approaches had been tried with no positive change in the breeding shed. The vet was running out of options and thought there was nothing to lose if I worked with this stallion.

When I approached Campy's stall, he stood in a corner with his head down and a worried look in his eyes. He barely looked up when I spoke quietly to him. I opened his stall door and telepathically asked his permission to be with him. Campy was very hesitant at first as he was surprised a human could hear him. I did not push, but sat quietly on the waterer while he got the feel of having a human listen to him. When he relaxed and opened up, he was very clear in what he wanted to show me.

I brought - expert place. I unable perform - job breeding. Much upset home place - expert place.	expert place = veterinary facility
Problem many facets. Discomfort my body. Emotional frustration leading - lose confidence. Poor handling breeding shed. Stings. Pressure producing for my power human. Shoulders very heavy. Managed daily. Contact - lack contact other horses. Factors - collected my being unable release.	stings = shots, vaccinations power human = owner

Campy had a large booking for the season, representing a lot of money, which he did not understand. The necessity to breed was literally a big weight on his shoulders, so he was unable to release semen.

Head stallion human job finding why I no breed. Stallion human treat me kindly. I no forced - no handled roughly. Stallion human cared of me. I no on list. Tries no success. Stallion human - see piece missing. Stallion human - frustrated - ask mare human expert place - listen of me. Human mare head talker.	head stallion human = veterinarian A picture of all the stallions this man was treating, with the sickest at the top of the picture and the least sick at the bottom. human mare head talker = author
Mare human come my stall. Humans listening - important. Humans talk of us - seldom listen of us. Show mare human - frustration - body discomfort - pressure breed many mares.	
Show mare human message of stallion human - my appreciation of stallion human working of me. Want stallion human know I feel caring him to me. Feel caring of my power human. Stallion human makes difference of stallions work with.	

Mare human hear of me. Being heard helped me move sadness - frustration out. I feel lighter - less burden my shoulders. I asked I want continue breeding stallion? I show willing continue. My no able breed no - no wanting breed - no refusing breed. Important clear.

Stallion human shown - I show mare human. Stallion human adjustments given of me.

His inability to breed was not because he did not want to breed and he was not refusing to breed.

There were changes made in the veterinarian's care of Campy.

The second time Campy was taken to the breeding shed after having been listened to, he was able to release semen. The worried look was gone from his eyes and he no longer stood with his head down in the stall. When I came to his stall, he came right to me. After a few more successful sessions in the breeding shed, Campy was sent home with everyone thinking the problem was solved.

Once home, the situation quickly deteriorated. He again could not release semen and was sent back to us within seven days of leaving. I was called to work with him because no one could find anything physically wrong. Disappointment hung heavy in the air, both for the veterinarian and myself.

Disappointment - expert stallion human - mare human head talker - I feel. Mare human come my stall. I show mare human want do my job breeding.

Problem handle of me breeding place home. Human handling me - heavy hand - metal snake. Upset me - disrespected - unfair. No able release semen.

Mare human hear me. Mare human show expert stallion human. Expert stallion human handle me breeding place soft hand - respect. Job breeding easy.

Being handled with a quiet, gentle hand in the breeding shed was all Campy needed to go back to doing his job. The decision was made to have Campy stand the rest of his breeding season at our facility. After the breeding season was over, the veterinarian went along when Campy returned home to show the owner and handler how Campy needed to be handled in the shed.

I have learned from working with horses that emotional issues and/or stress can sometimes be the cause of their problems. This, along with physical pain, was the case with Campy. For the breeding season of 2005, Campy stayed home, doing his job easily. It was a happy ending for all concerned.

Smokey

Quarter Horse stallion.

Smokey was a champion cutting horse. He sustained an injury while cutting that ended his career. The decision was made to use Smokey for breeding, and he was sent to a breeding farm to stand at stud.

July 9, 2004

One day I passed Smokey's stall, and he looked at me so intently I stopped to see what he wanted. Smokey immediately showed that he wanted me to get him out of there so he could go cut cows. I explained to him I was a low herd member and did not have power in the human herd to do what he wanted. All I could do was tell the barn manager how Smokey felt.

Wanted told stallions miss job. Humans give job - breeding stallion. *Humans no ask me want stop job.*	Some stallions miss the job they did before breeding.

I miss cows. Keeping cow away other cows. I watch cow - no listen human on my back. I know job.

Want humans know some us miss jobs. I angry.

Smokey was angry with all humans. His head could snake around very fast, and he would have grabbed me with his teeth if he got the chance. I never turned my back on Smokey, being careful he never got that chance.

King

Thoroughbred stallion.

July 20, 2004

I had stopped going to see the horses because my old fear—doubting myself—had resurfaced, as it does from time to time. However, the horses kept asking me to come back. One day in my car, I found myself making the turns to take me where the horses were. I stopped fighting and went. When I arrived, I sat and listened by a pen of mares, writing for about an hour. When they were done for the day, I headed for my car when I heard King, a former A-circuit show jumper, asking me to come to his pen.

I walked the distance to his gate, and he immediately came over to me. I rested my hands on the mesh, and he pressed his muzzle against it to touch me. King was trying to tell me something, but I could not understand what he was saying. It was frustrating since I could feel he was sad and upset. I quietly stood with him. Then he showed he wanted to give me something for the stallion chapter. I was surprised, as I thought the stallion chapter was complete. I told him I would come back and he could have his say. I hated to leave him and wanted to go in to stroke his neck but didn't trust myself to do it. I would later regret not comforting him. Why is trusting myself so hard?

July 21, 2004

I received a call from my friend at the breeding farm. She said King had injured himself badly. He had apparently fallen while sparring with another stallion over a ten-foot high fence. The veterinarian had been called and she was waiting for him to arrive.

King immediately came into my head and asked me to come. I told her King's request, and she asked me to come out. As I drove to the farm, I could feel King. He showed me he would not recover from his injury, and he wanted to "go."

When I got to his pen, the barn manager told me there had been a decision to sell King because he was releasing urine into his semen, making it unusable. That was what he had been trying to tell me yesterday. He rested his head against my chest and asked to be let go. I told the barn manager what King was asking.

It seems there are no accidents. What I felt from King was that he couldn't face being sold, so he created an event that would allow him to leave. He showed me that he had torn an artery internally. Externally he was bleeding from both nostrils. He could not put weight on his left hind leg. I stood with him in his pen while waiting for the vet to arrive. The following is what he had to say…

Stallions no niche have. We labeled - bad - we no behave way humans want. I one these.	Some stallions don't fit in if they don't behave in the way expected.
I liked job jumper. I frustrated - no humans saw me - who I am. Trouble I discomfort of my feet. Metal devices uncomfortable. Human of metal devices - kind human - do humans best.	metal devices = shoes human of metal devices = farrier
Jumping ended - I taken humans place of stallions breeding.	

Miss jumping. Humans of stallion breeding place see who I am. I behave no well. Head mare human saw me of no meanness. Simply no behave well. Head mare human know I no injure human - intently. Young mare humans care of me - like me - especially tall young mare human. Tall young mare human kind of me. I like.

young mare humans = grooms

First time my life - humans see me - care of me. Hearts of young mare humans I carry me - I go.

He takes with him the kindness shown by this young woman.

I go = I die

Want humans know - no all stallions fit mold humans make of us. We intelligence - humans no see. We no behave humans idea - humans label us - bad. Goes troubled on - on.

Once a stallion is labeled "bad," humans see him that way forever.

Why humans no ask of us? Why humans quick label us? Label sticks - door closes of way looking of us. Why humans no see our side? Why humans no stop ask - us want? Why no humans listen? Humans talk much - over much.

Want humans helping of me - know I see humans good hearts humans caring of me. Humans speeded movement my leaving.

Humans help him leave quickly via euthanasia.

Want humans know - I peaceful. We experience discomfort different. We mechanisms different of humans.

No mistake of humans created my injury. Injury created of me.

My life no perfect of humans seeing. I see life good of me.

Ask humans look stallions fully seeing. Look beyond humans fear. Humans - See glory of us. Ask questions of open minds. Let go stiff images humans hold of us - against us.

My legacy - gift humans.

The vet arrived a few minutes after King stopped his images. After examining him, the decision was made to put him down. I stayed at his head while the vet prepared the shot that would end his life. King looked at me and thanked me for hearing him. I stayed at his head while the shot was given, careful to be out of the way when he went down. I knelt at his head, stroking him and telling him what a wonderful stallion he is. He peacefully took his last breath with a sigh.

CONSIDERATIONS

The stallions in this chapter were amazing horses with whom to work. I was awed to be in their presence. These stallions were not saying they did not want to do their job breeding. Rather, they were asking us to look more closely at how we house and handle stallions.

For whatever reason, I was not drawn to stallions that were with bands of mares and allowed to pasture breed. They were not the stallions whose paths crossed mine, and I trust that they did not have particular messages for this book.

The stallions I worked with in this chapter were in tightly managed breeding situations. These stallions were asking us to look at our fear when handling them. I once experienced moments of fear moving a stallion from stall to pen. He reared and waved his front legs in my face. It was hard not to overreact and jerk on the horse at a time like that. What was needed was to stay centered, calm and steady, using just the right amount of tension on the lead to get the horse to walk peacefully using all four feet. Handling stallions well is an art, and those of us who are not possessed with the talent are best not handling them at all.

The stallions are asking to partner with us more closely and to have a more active part in how decisions are made that affect their lives. For some people, this may be a tall order.

Working with these stallions, I found my point of view began to change. I developed a deeper awareness of them as fellow beings with whom I share the earth. I saw myself not knowing as much as I thought. I had a spiritual awakening which continues to unfold. At first this came as a surprise. When I started this book, I simply thought I would translate what the horses showed me. I did not realize the translation work would change my life in ways I could not foresee.

Chapter 2

Mares & Breeding

A horse band or herd is made up of mares, foals and youngsters. A mare's job is to procreate and raise foals. There is always one mare that is the lead mare of a herd, and she is responsible for leading the herd to water, grazing areas and safety. She establishes her dominance over all the other mares, foals and youngsters in the band. Her position is challenged daily, and she defends it until the time comes when, for reasons of age or injury, she is no longer able to maintain her role.

Lead mares do not fight the same way as stallions. The flick of an ear or the lowering of her head is all it takes to move another mare, foal or youngster away from her. If another horse does not respond to a subtle cue, then she will bite or wheel and kick until the other horse moves out of her space. Unlike the prolonged battles of stallions, the mare's behavior is short and retribution swift.

Lead mares tend to be older and wiser. They know where the best water and grazing are found and which areas to avoid because of a higher population of predators. Horses, being prey animals, are always on the alert for danger from predators. Herd hierarchy is established with the predator threat in mind. The horses have shown me the image of the herd in single file. The dominant, lead mare is at the head of the line with her foal, followed by each less dominant mare and foal, until the last horse in line, which is least dominant and the most vulnerable. No one wants to be last in the herd—they are most likely to be killed by a predator. This hierarchy is challenged daily.

In this chapter, I listened to mares in different situations. I heard what they wanted me to know about their individual lives. I'll let them take it from here.

Recipient Mares in Herds

A "recipient mare" is a mare with a healthy reproductive tract that is used as surrogate mother for an embryo obtained from a donor mare. Embryo transfer is the procedure by which mares are impregnated with the donor mare's embryo. It is done for a variety of reasons. The owners of a high-level show mare that want to continue showing *and* have a foal from their mare, may put her embryo into a recipient mare. Older, valuable mares that are no longer able to carry their own foals can have their embryos transferred into young healthy mares. Finally, a mare that has sustained an injury and is not capable of carrying a foal can still produce embryos, even if she can't carry the foal herself.

July 20, 2004

I was standing next to a pen containing 20 mares being used as embryo transfer recipients at a breeding facility. Many of these mares had been purchased in quantity from sale barns and wore numbers on their halters. Unlike the stallions, these mares were in herds in large pens.

Several mares immediately came to the fence and let me know they had things to show me. I sat on my folding chair and listened to them. At first it was hard for me, because they were all sending pictures at once. I showed them to slow down and let one mare work with me at a time. R331 stepped closer, looked into my eyes, and began to show me what these mares wanted humans to know.

R331

Grade Quarter Horse-type mare. Bay, no markings.

R331 was big boned with a stocky build. The way she stepped forward and stood slightly in front of the other mares made it very clear R331 was the one who would speak for the group. Her big brown eyes had an intelligent look as she gazed at me with intent, ears forward. R331 wanted me to take her home with me. I felt a tug at my heart, but realistically I could not take her, which I showed her. Being detached is important when I work.

We many locations come. No humans asked us we want come. We mares fell through cracks. We young. We together herd created of humans.

A picture of many horses and not enough humans to match each horse. Without a human, a horse can fall through the cracks of the human world and end up as surplus.

Our contact humans impersonal. Humans ideas of us - no who we are. We best cooperate.

We no understand why humans worried breeding rhythm. Why breeding mechanical? Broken compartments - segments - no seen whole of us. Why humans do - mystery of us.

It is a mystery to them why humans make it complicated.

We view creation foal one smooth uninterrupted movement. Movement of spirit. Humans need break apart - control - understand we function - confuses us.

Us perfectly flowing being. Our rhythms blend flow effortlessly. Movement - inner cycles - delicately balance.

Humans idea - form our bodies - made of humans desire specific form of function. Humans desire specific form of us - important of humans. We look no always balance function which humans breed of us.

form = shape
We have specific ideas what horses' bodies should look like within each breed. How a horse's body looks may not come up to human set standards, or function like we think it should.

Humans mind - separates humans self of heart - flow life. Humans mind - creates complications of us. Complications no ours.	

July 25, 2004

R331 came right over to me as I put my chair next to the pen. There were several other mares standing with her. Immediately she began sending pictures with an intently focused look on her face. Her eyes were bright with the excitement of being with a human who could hear her and was willing to pay attention.

Confusing know job of me? We connected group humans - no personal human.	They are working with humans but are not owned by a specific human
Young mare humans work of us. We paired young mare humans. Young mare humans learn foal creating. Young mare human paired of me no know hear of me. Young mare human kind heart. Young mare human no clear idea connection of me.	young mare humans = technicians
Young mare human does of me - iron arms place. I stand quiet - cooperate. I confused - things inserted inside me. Movement inside no comfortable.	iron arms place = stocks/chutes

A veterinarian will palpate a mare by reaching into her rectum with his or her arm in order to feel the uterus and reproductive structures underneath.

Tension young mare human - older taller stallion human speaks. Older taller stallion human - old stallion - seasons wisdom. Show young mare humans knowings.	older stallion human = male veterinarian

Hard of me young mare human tense.
Young mare human - being of me fuzzy.
I worry - I do something wrong.

fuzzy = the young woman is not clear in her mind

A technician was assigned to R331. This young woman got tense when being shown how to do procedures by the veterinarian, who was an older man. When this happened, R331 worried she had done something wrong to upset the young woman.

Why humans do things of us? Why no flow - horses are? Why young mare humans unaware who we are? Why young mare humans - disconnected of young mare humans thoughts. Why young mare humans - see separation humans - create humans of who humans are?

The humans were unaware that their unfocused thoughts were confusing the horses. Humans do not realize how aware horses are of human thoughts. Humans also separate their minds from their hearts or inner being. This is puzzling to horses.

We no opposed helping humans learn. We ask humans aware us - beings. We ask - no treated mechanically. We ask humans enter our bodies of us - carefully - respect of us.

We feel discomfort. We scared confined - iron arms. We confused bred humans way. We know foal spark alive. We know - is shock our bodies. Foal spark die rhythm cycle - foal no vital - our bodies balanced of event. Humans stings - we sick - no balance rhythm of us.

We moved our pen - strange pen - no all go. Miss friends. We moved - moving closed box - taken of place know. Go place no know. We buffeted by wind

foal spark die = aborted due to chemicals

Their bodies are balanced if the foal aborts naturally.

humans stings = drug injections

moving closed box = horse trailer

humans will. Humans no thought our wantings. Permission no asked - humans enter our bodies.

Humans reasons doings of us.

Humans have human reasons for exploring our bodies.

No presence our bodies - humans no explore. No learning young humans.

We ask humans explore us - awake. Conscious humans actions - thoughts. Aware consequences of us - humans doings.

The humans are not learning who these mares are as beings or understanding the mares' movements and rhythms.

The horses are asking us to listen and be aware that they are beings, not things. They are beings who have emotions, intelligence and the ability to communicate with us telepathically.

Life no clean - tidy - humans wanting so.

Exploring us done - numbers us go killing place. We no fear end life spark. We ask - treated respectfully - killing place. Humans learn kill - calm - respect of us. We give use our bodies freely. Use our bodies feed - life cycle of us.

Pictures of their bodies feeding wolves, coyotes, birds of prey in the wild—they are prey animals and this is part of their nature in the system of the planet. Rhythms of life entwining, where prey and predator are a natural part of earth's cycles.

Bodies born - bodies die. We rhythm life. Why humans no remember?

We ask humans - humans want know exploring of us? Why important of humans? What unknown of us humans search to know? We curious.

We no refuse. We work humans partnership. We ask - respect of us.

The mares were curious what humans wanted to know about them that the humans search so hard to find out. To the horses, life is rhythms that flow easily. Horses don't need to know about the technical details.

R277

Draft mix mare.

July 27, 2004

When I stood by the fence that day, a big chestnut mare approached me. She looked at me and then put her head over the fence. I offered the back of my hand for her to sniff. I had not noticed her before. I sat down on my chair, while she continued to look at me, ears forward. She stood at the fence alone with the other mares standing well back.

Humans no see us individuals. We no names - we wear marks our bodies - humans placed. *I ask humans - show gratitude job we do. Appreciated - acknowledged - job easier of us.* *No name - feel invisible of humans. I form - feeling - thoughts - being.*	There is a letter and numbers on tags attached to the halters they wear. These mares also have a freeze brand letter and numbers that match the tag.

R227 stopped showing me pictures, gave me a last look and walked away. I, as a human, felt chastised by this mare. She made it very clear to me she knew she had no name, that she felt invisible to us, and that she was not seen for who she was. It was true; I had not noticed her at all until she came to the fence that day.

R206, R230, R331, R342, R351

R277 moved away, and five more mares, R206, R230, R331, R342 and R351 came up to the fence taking her place. Their earnest faces touched my heart. R331 again took over, knowing I would get flooded with pictures because of too many horses sending at once. She showed me what these five mares wanted me to see.

We of service humans. Herd living - confined place - benefit us. Herd living comfort us. Humans use us iron arms place - return herd - comfort us. Comfort our bodies moving together. Freedom be horses together. Behave horse way. We act according - rank of us - of herd. Higher rank herd - move lower rank herd.	After being in the stocks, returning to the herd of mares was comforting for her and them as well.
Freedom be horses - benefit service - give humans. Freedom movement herd - keeps us whole. Confined separated herd harder of us - service give.	confined = kept in a stall
Humans no consider benefit us herd living. Humans use easy way of humans care of us - humans less work. Humans no think of us - outside humans wants of us. We no angry. Want humans think of us. Simple.	
Some us want - own human. Go own human - place. Own human protect us.	
Some us - content - remain service of humans. Living herd - no humans riding us - suits us.	
We temperaments. Shy. Very smart. Sad. Accepting. We no see us - victims. Choice our part. May no look way of humans thinking.	
Leave we choose. We create no repair injury - humans release.	leave = die humans release = euthanize
Falling sky water saturates earth we stand on. Saturated earth - cover our bodies. No pleasant feel long suns. We endure discomfort our bodies - of service humans. Is so.	They are standing in mud. Pictures of being in large open areas where they can move when it rains, so they are not standing in mud. long suns = long period of time
We no see us - lower workers. Our service - no less important - of dressed up horses.	Pictures of horses with saddles, blankets, showing, racing, etc.

The mares enjoyed standing near me while I wrote what they showed. They knew I was hearing them. I see these mares as generous beings, gentle souls whose service is given to us freely. I am honored to be in their presence. Their peace of spirit flows over me, and I drink it in. I aspire to their level of peace within myself.

Recipient Mares in Stalls

September 24, 2004

It took almost two months for me to return to listen to the mares. I was learning to trust the horses to create the time when I worked with them, and to stop worrying when nothing happened for a while. My work happens at the horses' pace, not mine.

There were mares in stalls with outside runs that could see each other and touch through the fence. These were additional recipient mares who were each carrying another mare's embryo and would raise that other mare's foal. The mares came to their fences and, once they understood I could hear them, they started sending me pictures.

Humans no ask us - want grow foal? We bred - human dictate.	
Job growing foal - big responsibility. Humans forget.	
In herd we interaction - comfort other mares. We protection - breeding energy herd stallion. Stallion energy balance mare energy.	They have the protection of the herd stallion.
Live humans boxes - lose balance life.	live humans boxes = live in stalls
Movement foal enters earth herd mares hold welcome. Mares energetically create safe circle energy - foal enter of. Foaling mare intent job - releasing foal of earth. Foaling mare inward - her focus. Herd	movement foal enters earth = birth

mares hold outer focus. Balance formed inner - outer.

Rhythm birth movement simple of us. Mare - foal move dance - rhythm each holding part.

Mares body - moves foal. Foal begin - waking up. Readying foal separation bodies. Foals body systems quicken.

Moment release - followed waiting quiet. Herd holds - quiet space. Herd collective breath held - released foal touches earth. Herd follow ancient rhythm - life arrived. earth sends energy through foals body. Herd sends waves energy - new member.

moment release = birth

Foals first breath - movement body rhythm. Mares body responds release - mares rhythm. No rushing - pushing. Rhythms within rhythms - move effortlessly. Our horse nature - being. We follow lifes - now movement. Moment - movement.

Horses live in the moment, letting things occur as they come.

Our thoughts - now. Now - unfolds us. Each member herd holds place pattern. Each herd holds own pattern. Matrix each herd member - creates pattern. Patterns infinite as matrix herd member. No two matrixes alike.

Each herd member holds an individual vibration. Then each herd has its own vibration pattern made up of the combined vibrations of the members of the herd. No two vibration patterns are alike. Vibration is the best word I can use to describe what they showed.

Movement our bodies - unending flow - creation moment.

Human contact - alters our flow. Contact - by our agreement.

Release foal sharper edges - in human boxes. Human thought currents - interrupt flow release foal. Human emotions disrupt

release foal sharper edges = having a foal in a stall

human thought currents = humans worrying

flow - movement.

Human boxes - curtail our movement. Boxes - separate us. Breaking rhythm herd support. Release foal human way thought creates discord of us. Our bodies work harder. We feel exposed - less safe.

human way thought = way of thinking

Humans push us - rush us. Humans touch foal - too soon. We horses. Foals baby horses. Foal different - human babies.

Why humans touch foal immediately of birth - make foal human baby? Why humans sharp thought patterns? Why moment foal release no honored quietly? Why humans thoughts no respect horse way - foal release? Why humans sharp thoughts life rhythm horse way?

humans sharp thought = fear

Those mares were extremely upset when they were showing pictures of a human imprinting a foal immediately after its birth. I felt their upset so powerfully that I was almost sick to my stomach at the trauma and overload those foals experienced in their delicate systems so soon after birth. The word "rape" is an appropriate equivalent to what I saw in the mares' images. I remembered six years previously I had helped imprint a foal and now have deep regrets for having done it to that foal.

We follow unfolding rhythm. Unfolding rhythm breathing - no breathing. Simple. No breathing - no breathing body. Spirit breathes always. We live. Foal no breathing - watch spirit float away. Earth take body back. Life rhythm moves on. Why humans forget?

breathing = life
no breathing = death

Why humans force our bodies grow foals? Why humans sting us with strong liquids? Sting liquids - cause our bodies unbalanced. Our stomachs feel tight. Our inner rhythms distort - no rhythms unfolding way of us.

Humans wanting - treating us so?

strong liquids = drugs, vaccines

The mare is not being allowed to follow her natural inner rhythm.

Foals created humans way - less strong vital spark. Foals created humans way - bodies less flow rhythm of us. Less flow rhythm - creates break down systems. Body breaks down - faster. Body functions - less brilliant - alive.

We hold levels life our bodies - according level - humans dictate upon us.

The level of their vital spark is in accordance to what humans dictate to them with drugs, artificial insemination or embryo implants.

I was stunned by the power of what these mares revealed. After they stopped showing images, I sat quietly in my chair, looking at them in wonder. What words could I add to what they have so eloquently shown me? None.

CROSS-BREEDING

Cross-breeding is the intermixing of different horse breeds. It is included in this chapter since it pertains to breeding.

Lance

Andalusian/Thoroughbred gelding. Gray. 4 years old. 17 hands.

November 6, 2004

Another block of time had passed. During that time, I spent three weeks in New York while my Dad was dying. His funeral was November 3rd. I was at a friend's farm spending time with her horses, recharging myself before flying back to Colorado. Her farm was a haven for me in those last weeks. I would visit with her horses, and when they showed me images, I wrote them down. They helped me stay calm during the hours spent at the hospital with my Dad. All my life, horses had been my solace in times of difficulty, a blessing for which I am thankful.

The training work with Lance had been going slowly. He had a very difficult time focusing, and my friend was wondering what might be happening. Lance had no unwillingness or naughtiness in him, just a sad, depressed look. My friend had a caring, kind way of working horses and was always patient. Since she took time to work at their pace, we did not think there was a problem with the training techniques.

My friend was working Lance in the round pen. I was sitting on a barrel outside the pen watching and listening. They worked for about ten minutes, then Lance stopped in front of me and looked at me through the fence. He started showing me images. They did not have the clarity I saw in other horses, but were out of focus, slightly distorted and moved out of sync. Had I not had a lot of time with other horses learning how to translate, it would have been very difficult for me to understand this young horse. It was slow going for me, but he was so intent. Lance showed me images until I understood. I sensed the urgency from him that I grasp what he was sending me about being a cross-bred.

Some us - hard lives. Lines within us too close together.	The lines, or what I call wiring, are too close together, causing problems. The lines of breed characteristics are not blending well.
Dam - sire - different families - horse shape. Humans mix families horse shape - hard of us. Some mixes go well. My mix no go well.	horse shape = breed
My mind no function smoothly. World around me moves too fast my senses interpret. I lost in maze - scrambled images. I no want be this way. Mix families create me this way.	

Why humans mix us - little conscious awareness. We ask humans - carefully consider mix families. We no say - all mix bad. We ask humans - breed mare - stallion - awake - aware - conscious place of humans. Humans ask - we show humans good mare - stallion mix - no good mare - stallion mix. Humans - no ask. Want humans ask.	
My lack concentration - no humans showing problem. Is problem unbalanced mixing families - unbalanced core group.	No problem with the training. core group = gene pool
Some humans help - repair. My imbalance - mixed families - no repairable.	
Me dying preferable - living world swirling around me. I no able bring world - focus. Frustrating of me - I kind being - locked body dysfunctioning - distorted.	It is frustrating for him to be locked in a dysfunctional body with a distorted perception of the world around him.
I ask humans slow down - ask questions - search hearts - breed mare - stallion - mixed families.	
Humans heart - source. Human mind - poor source - answers.	
Humans I live place - caring. Understand - I no bad horse. Humans help me. I grateful.	
My body thin - bodys way - correction. Thinness enables me less whole. Less whole state I become very un-whole - die. Is no bad way.	Being thin is okay. It may help lead to his death.
My gift humans.	

At this point, so early in his life, Lance was leaning toward leaving, as it was so hard for him to learn what he was being asked to learn. Also, he did not feel well in his body. Life for him was a daily struggle to perform the simplest things. It was a blessing he was with my friend, who could give him the patience he needed.

What this young horse showed me made me stop and think about cross-breeding, to which I had never before given a thought. Even though his pictures were not very clear, he still came across in a powerful way. The message I received was to be more conscious of the possibility of dysfunctional consequences when cross-breeding. The horses are willing to let us know what works and what does not, if we will listen. We can learn to listen, if we are willing to slow down and take the time.

Donor Mares

A donor mare is a mare that provides her genetics in the form of eggs or embryos.

I had not been to see the mares in a long time. The mare chapter was not finished, and I was drawn to go see them again. When I allowed myself to move with their rhythms, it worked effortlessly. The mares were teaching me that following their movement was easier than my worry and frustration.

Rose Bud

Quarter Horse mare. Chestnut, white blaze. 27 years old.

December 21, 2005

Rose Bud was a shy mare who looked younger than her years. Bred from top bloodlines, she had a successful career on the track. Any fast movement, however, sent her quickly away.

I parked my car and was drawn to the barn where Rose Bud and many other old donor mares lived. I put my chair next to her pen. She came over for a sniff, and then stood quietly, working with me.

Hard come here. No humans prepare me - come. Taken place of knowing. Miss horses know. Hard of me.

Suns - moons - seasons here. Why I here?

I show her she is here to create a foal, which another mare will carry and raise.

Why humans create foal I no grow inside me?

I also show her she carries blood lines from which her owners want to continue having foals and humans perfected a way another mare can carry her foal.

Horse way - mare no grow foal - no foal. Horse way - mare whole grow foal. No whole body - no grow foal. Mare whole strong - grow whole strong foal - growing of mare.

Why humans stretch lines of us? Why stretch lines of mare - lines ended?

Mare - lines ended - accept no grow foal. No force grow foal - herd living way. Mare no make scent of foal creating - stallion no breed.

Mare no whole - create foal - foal no strong of vital spark.

I old body. No want foal. Humans push my body - force movement with stings. Why humans push?

Want go place know. Be old horse. Simple. No stings. No pushing.

Why humans no ask - wanting of me?

What Rose Bud wants.

Tired now.

Rose Bud showed me a picture of lines that was her individual life-line. A horse's life-line and vital spark are interwoven into the tapestry of life. Humans call them bloodlines. She is curious why humans want a foal from her when her ability to carry her own foal has ended. For Rose Bud, her line is at an end. Her ability to pass the vital spark to a foal has ended in her horse view of life. I saw sadness in Rose Bud's eye. She reached over the fence with her head. I offered her the back of my hand, and she pressed her muzzle into it. We shared a quiet moment before she walked away. I stood there thinking about what she had to say.

Then I saw the mare in the next stall trying to catch my eye. I was not finished yet.

Lady's Dream

Saddlebred mare. Black, star.

Lady's Dream was an elegant mare with big intelligent eyes. She had lovely stall manners and was nice to work with. Her pen was next to Rose Bud's, and when she caught my eye, she immediately started showing me pictures.

I miss past - moons - seasons. I important job. Humans excited - I best horse. Waving flower - shiny metal.	waving flower = ribbon shiny metal = trophies
I like humans excited. I like move fast - flashy. Humans confined - fancy place.	fancy place = show ring
I like noisy humans.	noisy humans = clapping, shouting
Humans - no excited. Humans - no take me - fancy place. No waving flowers. No noisy humans.	Her owners stopped showing her.
I do wrong? Why humans no touch me same way? Miss noisy fancy place.	
I bored. Stand small confined place. Humans take me - iron arms place. Why humans take me? Why humans push inside me?	push inside me = palpate I show her the humans want to have a foal from her.
Why humans create foal - disconnected movement way? We continual movement. Why humans see disconnected movement way? No see me. No hear.	disconnected movement way = embryo transfer
I want go home. No foal of me disconnected movement way.	
Why humans single focus?	

Want humans ask me - I want. Want humans see - continued movement - horse way.	Humans do not see the fuller picture.
I cooperate. Humans no bad heart. Ask humans - ask me. I serve quietly. Sad. Miss home.	
What important of humans? Use us humans way? I ask?	

I did my best to show her why it was important for her humans to have a foal from her. It still didn't make sense to her. There wasn't any more I could do, so I thanked her for her message.

As I turned and walked to my car, I noticed two mares, Bold Girl and Looking Spicey, in adjoining pens on the opposite side of the barn. They were shaking their heads at me, and Bold Girl nickered. I wanted to leave, but Bold Girl was persistent that I listen to her. There are times I feel like a horse slave. It's humbling.

I laughed and re-opened my note book.

Bold Girl

Quarter Horse mare. Gray.

Bold Girl and Looking Spicey came from the same farm. They were friends that the barn manager was very careful to keep next to each other. Bold Girl was tough and did not give much away. When she looked at me, I felt very insignificant to her. I was surprised when she approached me, as I did not expect it from her. I felt honored she would work with me.

Humans see my front legs. Humans make sad face. No sad face - I ok. My legs carry me. Legs carry - I survive. Legs no carry - I no survive. Simple.

Her front legs are badly bowed at the knees.

I no focus - legs. I adjust - legs crooked - is so. Humans - push me young. Bones no fully formed. Humans - big push - young body. Legs - bow. I adjust. Learn use body crooked way. No sad. No mad. Is so. I live - simple.

Humans no ride. Legs crooked. Good - no ride. I like no ride.

I come herd member. We together - always.

Humans - ok make foal of me.

Is stupid humans way - mind - sees us.

Stupid is the best word to fit the image.

My life ok here. I relax. Hard hold old life pictures. Old life gone - humans decide.

She let the old life go.

Humans - good hearts here. No understanding - horse ways - of foals.

I teach humans - no listen. Humans no listen us - mostly.

Why humans minds forget horse ways? I noble mare of my lines. Humans want foal of me. Humans take. Foal my body - humans seeing - good lines. Spark vital. Spark weak - humans take way.

A foal carried in her body produces better vital spark. When foals are made the human way, the spark is weak.

Humans learn sun - moons - seasons - foals human make way - weaker spark. Humans - no learn now.

No pity sight of me. I strong. Accept life - humans way - place.

Important mare - herd member - stay of me. Company. Humans barrier separate us.

I settle - humans way - long suns passing. No settle humans ways - life sad.

I smart. I settle. Life easier.

Humans power - bigger - our power smaller. *Is way of life. Smart ones of us - settle - flow humans way. No bad. Worse no settle. Fight for old ways. No good.* *Why humans want foal old body mare? Curious.* *I show head talker mare human. Head talker mare human show other humans. Gift. Better then foal of me.*	gift = this book

Looking Spicey

Quarter Horse mare. Palomino, blaze, right hind sock.

Looking Spicey was a feisty old mare. I had to be careful she did not run me over when the door to the outside pen was opened in the morning because she was going outside—period. She clearly was friends with Bold Girl. They would stand side by side at the fence between their two pens. Looking Spicey had a sweetness about her. She enjoyed an occasional grooming and stood quietly, seeming to enjoy the attention.

Bold Girl - I sisters. *I ok - here place. We support each other.*	Her relationship with Bold Girl is like sisters, but not related by bloodlines.
Best live same pen. No humans barriers between us. Why barriers now?	Bold Girl and she shared one of the larger pens for a while. barriers = fence
Why move us? Humans - no ask - want move. We like together place. *Big movement - we together. I - ok here.*	Important to them they are together.
Humans thoughts - scrambled - creating foals old body. Why humans scrambled thoughts? Why humans - no see - foal creating rhythm movement - soft unbroken	

- whole movement of us. Humans thought way - harsh - divided - no whole movement.

Bold Girl - I show lead mare human pictures - best create foal. Lead mare human - no see - our pictures. Lead mare human - see human pictures - inside head. No see our pictures. Why humans forget our pictures way talking?

Why have humans forgotten telepathy?

Humans long suns - moons - seasons passing know - see our pictures. Humans head rhythm - lose picture movement - slow long suns moons - seasons passing.

A long time ago, humans saw our pictures. Slowly, over a long period of time, humans lost the ability to see our pictures.

Head talker mare human sees our pictures. We ask head talker mare human show pictures of us - humans - no see pictures.

Humans - forget - us beings of spirit. We know rhythm life. We know rhythm movement - strong foal create. Humans forget.

Ask humans remember.

I - cooperate of humans. Show pictures - helps humans remember. I like show pictures head talker mare human. Feels good.

Bold Girl - I teachers - horse way.

Tired now.

It was a hoot to work with these older mares. They had a lets-get-down-to-it attitude, and the pictures were clear and easy to see. They obviously had a hard time understanding why the humans wanted foals from their old bodies. For them, creating foals this way was not in keeping with their inner rhythm of movement as horses. Yet, they did their best to accommodate the humans who worked with them. Their noble graciousness touched my heart.

CONSIDERATIONS

I was drawn to work with mares that were managed in artificial and manipulative breeding programs. My sense is that the horses wanted me to be with them in those settings because it was most important to them at that point in time.

There are many more mares living with private individuals, on small farms or on large ranches that are a part of breeding programs without as much human intervention. I was not drawn to be with those mares. That is something that may come in the future.

To me, it feels as if the horses are opening a door for us to look through, to ask us why we are doing these things to them. They are curious why we have to do so much. They are curious why we are afraid to let horses produce foals with less intervention, forgetting the natural way of horses.

We are being asked to remember that they are horses with a horse's way of being. They are herd animals, originally roaming large areas to find food, water and shelter. I am not sure how we can simulate this in a domestic setting. However, our awareness of their needs is still helpful. Horses are not asking to go back to a feral state. They are willing to be with and serve humans.

The mares are asking for a conscious partnership with us in our breeding programs. They want us to hear them, and in doing so, know how it is for them. I am learning they have great inner wisdom and awareness of what does and does not work for their bodies and their species. If we listen to them, we can make their lives easier, instead of simply dictating how it will be with no input from them or recognition of their effort.

Over the past ten years, I have learned with growing awareness, that horses never forgot how to use telepathy—*humans* are the ones who forgot. In our modern world, we are taught not to trust those inner "knowings" and, therefore, not to trust ourselves. The mares are asking us to remember that innate ability. I often explain to people they are hearing more from their horses than they think. I tell them to trust their gut feelings. Those gut feelings are from their horses.

We are being asked to see beyond our own wants and become aware of *their* wants and needs. We are being asked to see horses as beings with feelings and consciousnesses of their own. It is not that they do not want to serve us; they serve willingly and graciously. Some mares are willing to have a foal each year, but some want a job with a human and do not want foals. I see many mares struggling to do their jobs as brood mares. Some of them simply ask for acknowledgement from us for the job they do.

It certainly makes me stop and consider their questions. We have the ability to partner more with them and consider their needs more if we choose. I don't know what the answers are, but at least now we are aware of the horses' point of view. It is something to ponder and explore.

Chapter 3

Death & Dying

I had many opportunities to be with horses that were seriously injured, old or had a disease from which they would not recover. They had great acceptance of death and were much calmer about the dying process than the humans in their lives. The biggest problem for horses was the attachment and emotions people had toward them at the time of their deaths.

It would be easy to ignore or avoid the subject of dying, but the horses made it very clear to me they had things to show humans about dying. I could not exclude the topic because it was difficult for humans. The horses pushed me hard to include this chapter, and I finally realized it was my *own* discomfort about the subject that made me hesitate. Once the horses were finished politely kicking me in the derriere, I was happy to include it.

Over the years, I have learned much about dying by translating what animals had to say to their humans and by volunteering in a hospice program for people. I received detailed training essential for the caregiver in how the body shuts down when dying. I did not know at the time this training was preparing me for the work I would do with animals. Now, half of my translation work is done with animals that are dying. I feel privileged that they will work with me during this most important event in their lives.

Mermaid

Quarter Horse mare. Dark bay, no markings. 3 years old.

May 16, 2004

Sometimes horses have unexpected lessons to teach us. Mermaid was one of those horses.

Four mares, three to five years old, arrived for breeding at one of the barns to which I was assigned. They had been range-raised and were skittish and hard to catch. Mermaid was the youngest and was a maiden mare. She was shy but sweet and smaller and lighter than the other mares. I spent extra time with her and she seemed to like the attention.

The mares were scanned daily using a small ultrasound transducer that was inserted rectally to observe the ovaries. One afternoon at feeding, I noticed Mermaid looking depressed and not interested in her grain or hay. I notified my boss and the veterinarian in charge of the breeding and waited with Mermaid for their arrival.

Discomfort - mid line up towards the udder - right side.	
Depressed. Confused.	
Why I here?	I show her she is here to be bred, then sent home once the pregnancy is confirmed.
Why human hurt me?	I explain the examination is to help the human know if she is ready to be bred, and that there is no intent to hurt her.
No - go - home place. No - want be - here. No want foal - human way.	She does not want to go back to farm she came from.
No - sure - want stay - of body.	She is not sure she wants to stay alive.

I relayed what Mermaid showed me to the vet. He found a tear in the lining of the rectal wall on the right side, and a regimen of care was outlined.

No - happy my life.

When she showed me this, I felt sadness and a lump in my throat. I allowed this to move through me. When it had passed, she felt lighter and gave a big sigh. The lump in my throat and the sad feeling were gone.

Take me to you.

Tired.

She wanted me to take her home with me. I showed her I couldn't do this.

I left her. My boss and I took turns checking her throughout the night. Over the next ten days, Mermaid received constant care. It was an up and down time for her. Some days she felt better than others. Another crewmember and I spent as much time grooming and handling Mermaid as we could. She became easier to catch and seemed to enjoy our attention. A special turnout area was created to allow her to be out of the barn and see her friends when they were turned out during the day. Mermaid rallied and seemed to be getting better. We were all encouraged to think she would pull through.

May 25, 2004

Mermaid was quieter than usual during evening chores. She was eating and drinking, but something just did not seem right. The next morning she looked listless with blank eyes and no response to my touch. The vet was alerted and examined Mermaid. She had developed a systemic infection. There was nothing more medically to be done.

Mermaid's owner was called, and permission was given to put her down. I stayed with Mermaid while the preparations were made. I was very sad, and went over the last ten days in my mind, trying to see if there was anything I had missed that could have made a difference. This is what she showed me in that quiet time before the vet and assistants came.

No sad - small human.

I worked - to stay. My body - no repair. No repair - no stay. Simple.

Old home - no kind hands. Here - kind hands on me.

Old home - harsh voices. Gentle humans voices - here.

Old home - one of many. Here - chosen of many.

Peaceful - no sad going.

I take of me - kind voices - gentle hands - caring hearts of here - going away. Is good.

Know caring humans - here. No know - caring humans - old place. Make change of me - experiencing caring - kindness. Is good.

No sad - of me. Peaceful - of me.

I stood at Mermaid's head, and she gave me a look that had a smile in it. She showed that she was peaceful and was fine with leaving. I nodded to the vet that it was okay to proceed.

Mermaid went with a sigh, and I heard her say "thank you." She was gone. I did not feel sad. I was happy she had gotten something good out of what looked to be a painful situation to us, as humans. She taught me life is experiences, and we choose how we feel about those experiences. We can choose to feel bitter and angry, or we can choose to feel cared for by the kindness others have given to us.

Mermaid did not blame the human who had caused the tear in her rectal wall. She chose to see human concern for her, caring human hands on her body and gentle human voices in her ears. She worked hard to stay. When she couldn't stay, she accepted it graciously. Mermaid will hold a special place in my heart. She was a wonderful teacher.

Czar

July 26, 2004

Arabian stallion. Bay. Over 20 years old.

Czar, a former show horse, had severe, chronic laminitis. This is a very uncomfortable condition due to the swelling of the laminae and the ridged nature of the hoof wall. It is much like a bruise under a fingernail.

The story of how I came to be with Czar that evening was amazing to me. I continue to follow where I am led. I had gone to see a friend's puppy and she told me about the stallion that had been brought to the clinic that day. I could hear him immediately, and he asked me to come see him. He showed me he had things to say about dying, so I drove to the barn.

There are no words to adequately describe how I felt in Czar's presence—the power of his spirit was so strong as I wrote. I felt his peacefulness, even though his feet hurt. My mind saw a too-thin body with horrible sores, standing in a way to relieve the pressure in his feet. My heart saw a starkly different image—a beautiful, strong, wise spirit that shone through his eyes. Those eyes were filled with wisdom and love. Czar's spirit was alive and full of life—inside a body that was a wreck. I felt privileged to be in his presence and honored to be asked to sit outside his stall. Our horses have so much to teach us about life.

I stood at the bars of his stall. He pressed his muzzle through, and we blew into each other's nostrils. I reached in and stroked his neck, feeling his peace and calm. I experienced one of those moments of simply being in the now. Time stood still being with Czar. I knew I was standing in the presence of great kindness, empathy and love. I hesitate to use the word "love." What does it mean? Sometimes I am not sure. I know what I felt in the moment of touching his neck was very special. The word love is the closest I can come.

Czar asked me to tell his veterinarian what he was showing me. I wondered if I had the courage to do this. No human asked me to come here—I was asked by Czar. He was another wonderful teacher.

Know my body deteriorated. Discomfort my feet. Humans see me - think die - humans help - before now sun. No die now. No ready die. Sun - moon in body no complete.	He is very clear he is not ready to die, even though he does not look well and is in much pain. This came as a surprise to me.
Humans see suffering - we see life. Life of us no clean - no pretty always. Life messy. Fever - heat - pressure my feet - is. Experience - have now.	
Human mare bring me - blameless. Humans judge human mare harshly - how body is. Sores my hips. Thinness my body.	human mare = owner Pressure sores from being down and he is very thin.
Humans see - humans blame human mare. I see human mare - know caring of me. Human mare took me - compassionately. My heart called human mare - take me - human mare hear - human mare take.	His present owner took him on, knowing he had a history of chronic laminitis.
Mistakes - humans of knowledge. Mistakes - how life learned. Why humans fear messy parts life? Messy parts life - learning parts. Growing parts. Expanding parts.	humans of knowledge = veterinarians
Short circuit discomfort - shortens learning experiences - now.	

I peaceful. Know this. Worry - released of my body - before ready released.	The reason he asked me to come was to pass this information on to the veterinarian handling his treatment. The vet was planning on putting him down the next morning.
Human mare - I together - our walk together. Lessons learn - our lessons learn - walk together.	Czar and his owner have lessons to learn in their time together.
Humans afraid see. I no fear spirit rising out body. Worry - forced spirit rise out - no ready.	
Human mare - here - I released.	Having his human with him when he is put down which is what the vets are planning to do.
Discomfort - my feet - body - no touch spirit I am. Events body - enrich spirit I am. Humans miss - humans fear - spirit rise out. Humans fear - humans no control.	Humans fear not having control.
Life rhythm - many movements. Movements - soft - sharp - dry - wet. My life rhythms - experience of me. My right. Humans - learn listen rhythms. Listen - act according - asked.	
No formula spirit rise out. Individual - own rhythm - movement rising out body. Humans rush us. Humans dictate - horses rising out body. Humans - no dictate humans - rising out body. We ask - humans dictate - wisely. Use humans dictate - hearing us. No humans mind - mind no hear - no feel.	They want us to listen to their wishes and act accordingly.
No judge human mare. No know path human mare - I walk of us.	Humans don't know the path my owner and I walk together.
Some horses teachers. I am so. Wear ugly suits - our choice. Teaching is honor. Gift given freely.	

I went home and typed what Czar showed me. I telepathically told Czar I would share his concerns with the veterinarian taking care of him.

I drove to the barn early the next morning and gave the pages to the vet. I asked him to read this information before putting Czar down. It was difficult for me to do this, but I had made my agreement with Czar.

The vet read the pages, and Czar was given the extra days he wanted. On the fourth day Czar lay down, unable to get up, making it clear he was ready to go. He was put down later that day. He went peacefully, having had the time he wanted.

Trusting what I am shown in a case like Czar's is a challenge. Usually when I work, I am asked to do so by the animal's human. With Czar, he was the one who asked. It put me in a delicate place with the vet and the people managing the barn. Sometimes I walk a very fine line between the horses and the people involved. I do my best to be respectful of people's beliefs. I don't try to convince anyone that animals can communicate telepathically.

San Luis Valley Wild Horses

September 13, 2004

A friend of mine living in the San Luis Valley in Colorado was very involved with the wild horses there. She was concerned about the horses being hit by cars and possibly killed when crossing the road that divided the valley. She wanted me to show the horses to stay away from the road, so we went up to the large mesa where bands of the wild horses lived. I sat and began showing them to stay away from the road for their own safety. Several horses immediately started sending images back to me.

This was the response from these wild horses about our concerns.

We compartmentalize leaving. We movement of rhythm leaving body.

leaving = death

Humans idea - we no share. Human idea - suffering. We feel discomfort - no feel discomfort.

Body survival mechanism - own rhythm. Survival rhythm - preserve body life. Spirit - own rhythm - being. Spirit - always fine. Only body dies.

Humans see suffering - humans suffering - no ours. We live - rhythm life. No victims of us.

Predators job - balance numbers of horses. Humans alter - balance of all. Humans now predators - keepers of balance.

Horses leave - leave by permission. Humans forget life ups - downs - of balance.

Humans - unbalanced - view life. Humans - want - no mess. Mess - part life - in body.

The message these horses had to show was short and sweet. They were not worried about dying. They saw humans keeping the horse population in balance.

Alan

Quarter Horse stallion. Dun. 19 years old.

November 16, 2004

I was called by a barn manger who had heard about me. She asked me to come to their farm to see an older stallion who was not doing well. Their vet diagnosed colic and was not sure if there might be something more causing the symptoms.

The manager took me to Alan's pen. He was standing in the corner, head hanging down. I asked Alan's permission to enter his pen, which he gave. He barely looked in my direction as I walked in and stood quietly, six feet away. When I asked his permission to work, he raised his head a few inches and looked straight at me. It took a minute for him to open to me.

I asked the barn manager if there had been a change in Alan's standing. She said that even though Alan was easy to work with and a gentleman in the breeding shed, a decision had been made to sell him to make room for a new stallion. Alan had a dull look in his eyes. I sat in the corner, writing what he showed me.

I tired. Internal systems slow now. Imbalances of me - no repair.	He showed me his digestive tract.
Discomfort. Discomfort my muscles. Muscles poisoned.	His muscles felt tight, and to me, they felt toxic.
Feet discomfort - soles. Hard devices of my feet - too small - pinch.	hard devices = shoes
Small interest - my job - breeding. Small interest - be in body.	
I serve job well. Served humans.	
No want leave. Home is here.	He did not want to be sold and go to another farm.
Good suns - no good suns. No good suns - string together. Close of me - release my body.	He is getting close to dying.
No ready - now.	
My job done. Ask - humans honor - so.	
I no create - strong foals - now. Humans need see - important.	
Discomfort - abdomen.	He showed me an area of the large colon where dying tissue, the size of a silver dollar, was very thin and close to perforating.
Tired now.	

Alan turned away from me, faced the corner, and hung his head. I left the pen and told the barn manager what Alan had given me.

November 18, 2004

I received another call to see Alan. By 10 p.m. when I got there, he was down. I sat in the hay near him. He was lying quietly on his chest, bathed in moonlight on the chilly November night. I asked permission and immediately the pictures came. He was peaceful and calm as I sat with him.

The decision had been made to put him down the following morning. The barn manger wanted to make sure this was okay with Alan. I wrote by moonlight as the images flowed. It was a privilege to share this experience. My old doubts crept in. He looked me in the eye. He had things he wanted humans to know.

No understand. Humans want - foal creating fluid of me. My body - no balance. Fluid - no balance. *My body - no capable - creating strong foal. I incapable - joining with mare.* *Why humans - no see? Why humans - want foal creating fluid? Why take forcefully?* *No respect me - as being.* *Creating foals - humans way - weakens life force of whole.* *Collective life force - all horses - weaker now - humans interfering. Humans no see - our bodies break faster now - in recent season of cycles.* *Consider - humans actions - interfering.* *Foal creating - sacred trust. We ask - humans treat - respectfully of us. According natures rhythm - creating foals.*	foal creating fluid = semen

I asked him if he was in pain.

<table>
<tr>
<td>

I feel discomfort. Discomfort - no enemy. Friend. Discomfort - force - me move. Movement - break - weak point - abdomen. Breaking - release me - of body.

Dying own dance - of movement. I want release. No stop - discomfort. Discomfort - allow - leave body. Leave body - expression - spirit growth.

Humans hearts - intent help. Humans need learn - see help - many forms. Gift - I leave - humans.

I taught well.

</td>
<td>He was asking us to see that help comes in many forms, and for him, discomfort was a friend that would speed his release.</td>
</tr>
</table>

Alan was put down early the next morning. A necropsy was done to determine the cause of his illness. The veterinarian found an area with diseased tissue in the wall of the large colon. It was the size of a silver dollar and so thin it was about to rupture. Knowing this helped me enormously. Alan had told me I could trust what I was seeing, but it was still hard for me. Getting this confirmation helped me to continue what I do.

Sitting with Alan that night was one of those perfect events where time stands still and I was in the moment. I was sharing it with Alan, a wonderful being dressed in a horse suit. I am truly blessed.

Pokey

Quarter Horse gelding. Bay, no markings. 30 years old.

April 1, 2005

Pokey lived on the small ranch where I lived. He had been there a long time. When the ranch was sold 20 years before, he came with it.

He was sweet-natured and a joy to be around. His pen was right outside my front door, and he was a great neighbor.

I knew Pokey was getting close to dying. In the past few months he had slowed down noticeably. He was not eating much, had a harder time getting up, and was not as steady on his feet. He did not live with the herd because the young ones pushed him aside.

I was getting ready for a month-long trip to the East Coast, so I spent some extra time with Pokey. He had things to show me, and I sat with him while I wrote.

I old body. I simply am. Old body slower rhythms.	
In wild - old horses - fall behind. Death - rhythm of life. How die no important.	
Body survival rhythm - works till - last breath taken. Survival rhythm - what body does.	
Body function - survive.	
Dying - takes as long as takes. Our spirit - sometimes leaves before last breath. Spirit moves on. Body shell.	body shell = the body is a shell
Old horse life with humans - out of rhythm.	
Humans want us live - no want dying. Humans give us stings. Humans give us - high food - energy matter. Keep body alive.	stings = shots
Why humans - no like old? Why humans - no want dying?	
Humans - push us out - body too soon. Is hard find dying rhythm - human care. Human mind forget - rhythm dying.	push us out = euthanasia
Humans worry - of discomfort. Worry - body struggle.	discomfort = pain
Is many levels comfort dying. Each horse - own level comfort - dying body.	
Some us leave - easily. Some us - hard leaving. Is as is.	

We no hold pictures - how dying - look. No - fix picture. Each horse - each horse. Ten horses - ten ways dying. Humans want - same way. Tidy - clean - no messy.	
We ask - listen of us. We let humans know - dying own rhythm best. Humans no like. Humans like - smelly humans come sting us - we die. Easier - on humans.	dying own rhythm best = not being put down smelly humans = veterinarians
Dying - part experience life.	
We ask humans - relax. See dying - part life.	
Humans relax - hold of us - dying easier - of us.	hold of us = emotional hold
Humans hold - on of us - dying - harder of us.	
See - dying rhythm - movement of life. Simple.	

Pokey gave me a look that said, “Got it?” and walked away. My experiences with my own animals dying were less traumatic when I was emotionally calm. When I was emotionally upset, it was harder on both sides. Being calmer made a big difference. It did not mean I loved them less.

Bright Morning

Quarter Horse mare. Chestnut, no markings. 10 years old.

Several mares had shown me it was really important to explain to humans about foals that die at birth. I remembered a mare I had worked with the year before who had lost her foal at birth. She gave me her permission to write her story.

April 21, 2005

Last year, Bright Morning's foal was born eight weeks premature, and nothing could be done to save its life. This year, she came to a breeding farm managed by a friend of mine, for constant observation during the last stage of her pregnancy. My friend asked me to spend time with Bright Morning, which I happily did.

Humans - watch. Why?	Humans are concerned her foal will come too early and are watching in case they need to help her and the foal.
Human of me - worry. Why?	Her owner really wanted her foal.
I grow foal - best of me.	
I miss - human gathering - show of me.	show of me = horse show
Growing foal - work. Boring.	
Want please - human of me.	She wants to please her owner.

Bright Morning was doing her best to grow this foal for her owner. She was finding it hard to be so closely watched and confined. It was four-and-a-half weeks from her due date. A foal arriving now would not survive as the lungs and hair coat would not yet be fully formed. Sophisticated equipment and nursing can aid the survival of a human premature infant, but not a premature foal.

It was late Sunday morning when I stopped by to see my friend and check in with Bright Morning. The mare was lobbying to go outside. The farm vet gave the okay, feeling the sun would do her good. He would be within shouting distance if needed. We turned her into a pen with shelter, let the vet know where she was and went to lunch.

When we returned an hour later, we were shocked and saddened to find Bright Morning had delivered her foal. It did not survive. We ran to notify the vet who was in the next barn. He, too, was shocked—having checked her just twenty minutes prior to our return. In that brief time, Bright Morning had delivered her foal.

The vet immediately removed the foal's body from the pen. Bright Morning was quite distressed by this. I tried to get the vet to leave the body with the mare for a while, but to no avail.

I stayed with Bright Morning. She kept looking around the pen for her foal. I did my best to show her the foal was dead. The following is what Bright Morning showed me about having a foal die at birth.

No human - emotion of us.	Their emotions are not the same as ours.
Humans - misread - our physical motions - death of foal.	
Our bodies geared - birth - nurture. Our hormones - support event.	
Foal dying - our bodies movement slowly shifts - birthing/nurture - to - no birthing/nurture.	
Sniffing - nudging foals body - sends signals - our center - reverse hormone action of birthing/nurture.	
Space - foals spirit lingers - readying float away.	space = at this time
Different levels attachment - to levels health of body - to space - spirit leaving.	Degree of attachment to the body and health condition of the body determine the time it takes for the spirit to leave.
Humans - rush us - take foal body away - before our hormones change motion.	
Taking foals body - disrupts movement - death. Affects us.	
Why humans - rush us? Why humans - no relax - allow - horse nature prevail? Why humans - afraid dead body - foal?	
We emotion - nurturing. Is different of human - emotion/attachment.	
We herd living - foal death rhythm - flows throughout herd.	When living in a herd, the death of a foal is felt in the whole herd.
Humans living - confinement of us - harder of us. No support - rhythm herd. Isolation. Separation. No herd support.	

Humans - no see - movement - rhythm - horse way. Is hard of us.

Hormones slower - shift away - birth/nurture movement. Herd move - away - body foal - foal spirit gone. Body - cools. Predators come. Simple - horse way.

Humans - take foal body - disrupt movement of us. Slower - our bodies recover. Empty - stuck - space of us.

Humans - no understand - rush us - rush us. Why humans - no feel - movement of us? Why humans - mind - see us - humans emotion way? Is different of us.

Picture of humans wearing shoes, living in rigid boxes. We are removed from natural contact.

We ask - humans leave foal body. Allow us - space - move horse rhythm - movement. Easier - of us. No stuck - our way.

We ask - hear us. Important.

The necropsy done on Bright Morning's foal showed a malformation of internal organs. Delivering her foal early was a natural conclusion—her body knew something was wrong. We humans were trying to keep the pregnancy intact.

I shared Bright Morning's images with my friend. She listened with interest as she was very committed to the well-being of the mares in her care. Bright Morning's message was that a mare's hormones need time to shift from the mode of beginning to nurture a live foal, to the non-nurturing mode when the foal dies at birth. Removing the foal's body from the mare's environment too soon disrupts and slows that hormonal change, making the process more difficult.

Learning where the balances are is a life-long lesson.

CONSIDERATIONS

The subject of death is huge for humans because it is so emotionally charged. It is simple for horses to accept the physical death of their bodies and the release of their spirits. It gets complicated because of the emotional bonds and belief systems of humans.

The important lessons horses have for humans about death are simple. In this chapter, the horses have clearly shown us they are not afraid of death. Death to them is part of life in a body. Their bodies are geared for survival, and the survival mechanism operates to the last breath. The survival mechanism is a very powerful force in all animals. Humans often confuse this or read this as "fear" of dying.

Horses' view of pain, what they call discomfort, is also part of life in a body. They see discomfort as a friend in the dying process, or what they call the "dying rhythm movement." Over and over they have shown me how discomfort helps shake the spirit to leave the body.

Horses are clear they have emotions, but not at the same level as humans. They do not have the same emotional component to death as humans do. They have a clearer, simpler view because they live in the moment. Horses are not thinking about the future like humans do. Their moment-to-moment living allows horses to move with the unfolding of life more easily. In this case, it is death.

It is important to mention that humans view life through what they are taught and what they experience. Each of us creates our individual filters through which to view life. If, for example, we have a view that all pain is bad, we will view through that filter. Using that particular filter, we then project that view onto whatever is going on in our lives at that time. In this case, a horse dying.

We, as humans, have our view of dying, and horses have their view of dying. In my many years of experience, I see they are different. Neither is right or wrong, simply different. By giving humans their point of view about death, the horses help create a bridge between us. It opens a door for us to see death slightly differently.

The three biggest things the horses want us to know about death and dying are:

1. A human's emotional attachment to his or her animal when the animal is dying makes it harder for the horse to leave. I saw this when my own horse died in 2003.

2. Humans tend to see pain as something to avoid. Horses see pain as discomfort and part of life.

3. Horses are not afraid of death—it simply is part of life for them. It is not an end, but continuous movement.

A whole book could be devoted to the subject of death and dying in horses. We have just scratched the surface in this chapter.

Chapter 4

Training

The small ranch where I lived had a group of young horses in various stages of "training." I was sitting by the fence with my pen and notebook wondering what topic to cover next, when these young horses came over. They immediately led me to understand they had things to show me about being "trained" and what it was like working with humans during this process.

In my years with horses, I have been in the role of a trainer. I personally prefer the word "school" or "schooling" instead of training. To me, training carries an image of dictate or force, while schooling is about asking, showing and learning.

The subject of horse training is huge. There are many different disciplines and ways humans use horses. While there are common threads that run through these disciplines, each discipline is a world of its own. Volumes of horse training books have been written since the time of Xenophon and the ancient Greeks, with more being written daily.

The current trend in natural training techniques has added yet another dimension. With advancing technology, we now have cassettes, videos and DVDs to explain and show how to train a horse. The amount of material and information available is so large, it tends to be overwhelming. This makes the horse industry both exciting and confusing, especially to novices and to the horses.

To whom do you listen? Let's see what this group of young horses had to say about "training."

Easter

Thoroughbred mare. Gray. 8 years old. 15.2 hands.

Easter lived on the small ranch where I lived. She was very intelligent and was being trained in the discipline of eventing. Even though she was an aggressive jumper, Easter was overlooked by prospective buyers because of her small size. People sometimes forget that good things come in small packages.

August 9, 2004

Easter looked at me and the pictures flowed.

<table>
<tr><td>Humans - create jobs of us. Jobs - many ways humans - use our bodies - jobs humans created. Jobs - meaning of humans. Big - of humans.</td><td>jobs = horse shows, polo, jumping, dressage, roping, etc.
Jobs very important to humans.</td></tr>
<tr><td>Humans - explain - our jobs of us - often no given clearly of us. Explaining gathering - we often confused - humans ask - want us doing?</td><td>Training often was not clear.</td></tr>
<tr><td>Explaining gathering - we receive pictures - our minds - moving boxes humans ride in - white boxes holding water moving around skins humans wear - flat surfaces inside boxes humans live in - upon which lie many white leafs with dirt on them. We no understand - pictures of humans. What pictures have to do - job humans explaining?</td><td>explaining gathering = training session.
What does the human want?
moving boxes = car
white boxes holding water = washing machine
flat surface with white leafs = desk with papers</td></tr>
<tr><td>Confusing of us. Our confusion - we do things - humans interpret us being bad. We bad - humans sting us - sharp stick. Scares us - confuses us - bigger.</td><td>bigger = more</td></tr>
</table>

Easter did not understand the images she saw in the human's mind when she was being trained. During a training session, without realizing it, humans are constantly sending images to their horses contrary to what they are asking the horse to learn.

Easter, Miles, Olympia, Alegra, & Chairman

Thoroughbred & Warmblood crosses. 4-8 years old.

August 11, 2004

I was with the same group of young horses.

We allow - humans use - our bodies - jobs humans create. Learning move how humans - want us move - our job - we have experiences - growing within - ourselves. Part spirit growth.

Learning - intricate movements - we experience - body movement flowing - effortlessly. Intricate movements - discipline - our inner being - allowing us - move beyond - instinctive horse behavior. Creating - confidence of situations - instinct us - run. Good feeling of us - achieve - higher levels knowing. Command - over - our instinctive behavior.

No all horses - achieve - level knowing.

Many levels - knowing. Many levels - intelligence. Humans - fail understand - no every horse - possesses - higher inner quality - move higher levels knowing.

Good training teaches horses to think their way through a situation, overriding their instinct to run to survive.

Few humans - quiet minds - creates simple clarity - showing us our jobs. Humans - quiet minds - easiest humans - of us - work with. We shown clearly - job asked - of us - helps us respond.

Few humans possess quiet minds. Ones that do are easiest to work with.

Clear thoughts from the humans help horses tremendously to understand what they are being asked to do.

We willing - work of humans. Humans confuse us - us no giving correct response - us unwilling - bad. Us - truly confused. Us no sure - correct response.

When the horse is confused and gives the wrong response humans label them bad.

Humans - send us pictures - explaining gathering. We no see - being asked of us. We flooded. Some us - handle flooded - better others us. We respond - we horses - use we know. Puzzles us - humans no understand - we saying of humans.

flooded = humans send too many pictures

Some horses handle being flooded better than others. Horses use the language they know.

It puzzles horses when humans don't understand what horses show humans.

We ask - humans - respectful of us - explaining of us. We ask - humans - respect our young - no fully - developed bodies. Why humans - push us - beyond our young bodies - capable? Why humans - push our - young minds beyond - our young minds absorb? Why humans - hurry - short moon cycles - takes many many - moon cycles - achieve? Why humans - no understand - slow steady unfolding - achieving - creates - achieving lasts many moons.

Humans compress what takes years to learn into too short a time.

many - moon cycles = years

Slow steady achieving - allows our bodies - develop strong - slowly. Why humans - acceptable - injuries sustained - of us - explaining gathering? Why humans - acceptable - break down - our bodies - before our bodies old? Why our bodies - pushed beyond - bodies limits? Why humans - jobs important? Why we - no same important? Why humans - throw us away - we damaged?

Taking the training more slowly creates a horse that is physically able to perform longer and better.

Why is it acceptable to humans when horses are injured during training?

The job is more important than the horse.

We ask - humans consider - questions. Puzzles us.

These are good questions to ask when working with young horses. It certainly stopped me in my tracks.

Easter & Headlight

Thoroughbred mare. Warmblood mare.

August 12, 2004

I was with some of the same horses.

Humans mind - needs taming - we no need taming - breaking. We willing - humans - forget.

Humans - no understand - power - humans minds - emotions. Humans - words - no meaning - of us. Thoughts - create - humans words. Thoughts - hold essence - intent - between beings. Thoughts - hold pictures. Thoughts - transmit emotion.

We open - easily - humans thoughts. Thought - coupled sharp emotion - comes through of us - forcefully. Feels us - being struck. Intensity - felt deep - our body.

Horses get slammed when we are in a highly emotional state. Our thoughts are open books to them.

Humans - unaware their thoughts - jumbled to us - explaining - our jobs.

Human thoughts are jumbled and not clear.

Humans - of clear thoughts - explaining of us - easy of us work - humans of clear thoughts. Clear thoughts humans - show us clearly - asking of us - do. We make mis-step of body - clear thoughts humans - stay clear - asked of us - do. Allow us - move - again. Correct movement - clear thoughts humans - praise us. We begin movement - do movement - correctly we asked - we grow confident - movement - grows easier of us.

Horses show how much easier it is for them to work with a human who has clear, focused thoughts, where they are not punished for a misstep and rewarded for trying, even if it is not totally correct.

We ask humans - be aware - humans thoughts. Humans - ask of us - clearly - helps us respond.

Humans unawareness - humans thoughts - surprise to humans.

It is a surprise to some humans, all the thoughts that are in their heads.

We want - humans know - our bodies move - new moving way - our bodies sore. We sore - hard move properly.

Humans ask - specific question. Is soreness? Humans - aware - helpful of us.

Humans - sit upon our backs. Is work of us - hold humans. Humans - holds well easier of us. Humans - no holds well - difficult of us - moved as asked.

Balanced riders are easier to carry than unbalanced ones.

holds well = balanced

Combine - thoughts jumbled - no holds well - is difficult - us move. Why humans blame - us first?

If humans have busy minds & are sitting unbalanced, this makes it difficult for the horse to move properly.

Humans - no of equal intelligence - same as us. Us understand - easier - us understand - slowly - us understand - very slowly. Humans - same way. We ask humans - consider - explaining of us.

Different horses, just like different humans, understand at different rates.

We cooperate - better - asked - cooperate.

Human - horse mix. Human - horse mix - effortless. Human - horse mix - no effortless. Humans - look - mix human - horse. Is - no bad human - no bad horse. Is - bad mix - no fault - human - no fault - horse.

Some horse/human combinations just don't work well.

Jobs - humans many jobs - of us. We like - dislike job. Some us - like our jobs - enjoying job of our human. Some us - no like job. Why humans - insist - we do job - no like? Why - no find job - we like? Is curious of us.

Humans have many jobs/disciplines for horses.

Horses don't understand when humans insist they do a job they don't like.

Movement - job we like - easy of us - less effort. Why - more effort - necessary?

Ease of motion - is flow of rhythm. Flow of rhythm - contains - harmony. Is no harmony - job of life? Consider.

Being in harmony is life's ultimate job.

Human - created devices. Humans place upon our bodies - affects our movement. Devices - no always - comfortable - wearing. We work greatly - do humans ask - human devices - hinder us. Humans - see flow - movement of us - create devices - work movement of us. Some humans - aware. We - grateful.	human devices = saddles, bridles, halters, etc. work greatly = hard
We acknowledge - humans aware - our needs. Humans efforts - our behalf - we welcome. *We waited - suns - moons - long cycles - our side expressed.*	Horses are grateful to humans that are aware of how the fit of equipment affects their comfort of movement.

What a lot of information to assimilate! I had been with these young horses, writing, for a couple of hours. When they stopped sending, they became quiet and content. A human had listened! It was important to them that I got their message. Working with them was great.

Young Horses

Thoroughbreds, Thoroughbred crosses & Quarter Horses.
Mares & geldings.

March 13, 2006

For the last few years, horses have been trying to show me how natural horsemanship "games" affect them. The horses were clearly revealing that it was important to them to have this subject included in their book.

This past week, the subject of games in the natural horsemanship movement came up in several different conversations. Each time, horses would come into my consciousness, explaining what it was like working with humans on these games. I had unhappy horses that

I had worked with periodically, come into my head showing me how it felt. I got a tight feeling in my stomach.

I have voiced to humans what their horses had shown me about games. So far, the messages have fallen on deaf ears. It is frustrating to know how the horses feel and not be able to do much about it.

Humans - pretense - games fun. Games of us doing - work of us - disrespect of us. Games - work us doing. Games - work our bodies - moving - way humans - want us move.	Humans assume games are fun for horses. Games are work for horses.
Humans - stuck - humans view. No - our view.	
Games. Stupid - our way seeing.	Stupid is the closest word to fit the picture.
Our view - playful movements - wrapped around - our survival.	From the horses' view, all movement is survival.
Humans - perception - playful movements - humans label - games - we do.	
Our expression - playful movement - life moving - feeling our body - survival. Free movement - of us - survival of us.	For horses life is movement.
Learning - body movement - skills - no game - of us. Body movement - skills - survival of us. Survival of us - our way - of being. No game. Why humans - no see - free movement - of us - survival of us. Game - humans view.	
Humans - disrespect - our movement - expression. Misunderstand - our expression. Human - mind - no listening.	

There was a lot of intensity to what the horses showed me regarding doing these games. They clearly felt disrespected. For them, the games had a different feel than when learning a job. It was a volatile subject with the horses, and a hard one for people to understand. The horses had clearly drawn a line between games and jobs. On the surface, horses do not seem resistant to games because they look quiet when participating in them. People tend to take that for acceptance.

The horses were clear that movement is survival. Survival is coded into their cells. We have our own interpretation about horses' movements. We should step back and take a look from their point of view.

What the horses showed me about games was powerful. It was more than about the games themselves. It was what the games represented, not just for the horses, but also for us. The games are a human concept belittling a horse's basic nature, which is movement to survive. When we do not value another being's nature, we are not valuing our own.

CONSIDERATIONS

I felt challenged on several levels as this book was unfolding. My life was changing, and the changes were not always comfortable. I looked deeper inside myself, exploring attitudes and actions. When I was with horses, I was more conscious of where my focus was, no matter what was happening. I found myself lacking, falling short of being the horseman I wanted to be. Working with the horses stirred up my past as well as my present. I remembered as a child wanting desperately to please my riding instructor and failing. Now as an adult, I face the fear of not making the correct response to a horse's needs.

The horses reminded me of our human attitudes. Do we approach horses with respect for their beingness, or do we demand whatever we want and expect them to perform? The next time I worked with a horse I examined my own attitude more closely and I was surprised.

Horses are asking us to be aware of where our minds are when working with them. Remember the human who was thinking about laundry while working with a horse? The young mare was receiving this strange image instead of the movement the trainer wanted her to learn. It was confusing to her. I was surprised when I began to have awareness of where my thoughts were when I was working with a horse. Very often I found I was thinking about doing the laundry!

I truly amazed myself when I started paying attention to where my thoughts were when working with a horse. The more I stayed focused on the task at hand, the easier the work went. I will not work with a horse now if I am upset or distracted. It takes discipline. The more I pay attention, the longer I find I can stay focused. It takes time and happens in little steps each day. Not one big step, *little* steps. I emphasize this.

I recently watched a young horse working in a bitting rig. What occurred to me at that moment was how humans want to force horses into a way of movement that we choose—not necessarily what's best for the horse.

How often do we stop to consider a horse's conformation? Are we aware of soreness as a possible reason a horse is not moving the way we want it to move? How consistent are we when asking a horse to work? Are we accurate or sloppy in our thoughts and actions?

Humans have ideas of how horses should move to fit a picture we've created. Horses are poured into molds we've built. Why is a horse called "stupid" when it is unable to move the way we "think" it should?

As I look back, I realize I need to apologize to horses I worked with years ago. My thoughts were scattered then. Now, I understand their generosity in working with me. What these horses gave is inspiring.

Chapter 5

Shoeing

The art of making and attaching metal shoes to horses' hooves goes back to ancient times. The skills needed in this process have evolved over many years with knowledge being passed from one generation of blacksmiths and farriers to the next.

An idea now emerging, along with the natural training techniques, is that of keeping horses barefoot. The natural barefoot trim is patterned after the wild horse hoof that receives no human care yet carries him soundly throughout his life.

Change always takes effort, and barefoot trimming has created a great deal of discussion, experimentation and research as to effectiveness. My early training in Pony Club and other teachings emphasized that putting on shoes was the only way to keep a horse sound in regular work. My views on this have since changed.

The horses themselves have been a major factor in my change of thinking by showing me how it feels to wear shoes. It's been a fascinating experience, even if challenging at times. Here is what horses have to say about shoes.

Gus, Larry, Safire

Gus - Lusitano/Quarter Horse gelding. Gray.
4½ years old.

Larry - Paint Horse gelding. Chestnut, blaze. 9 years old.

Safire - Thoroughbred gelding. Brown. 10½ years old.

October 20, 2004

I was in New York State at my friend Barbara's farm. I was taking a break from being at the hospital where my Dad was in ICU, and I did not want to believe he was dying. I needed some horse time. All of my life, horses have been my haven—giving me solace in times of sadness.

Barbara and her daughter, Amy, were sitting with me on a big bale of hay inside a shed. Amy was a natural hoof care practitioner, and the subject of horses' feet came up. A few horses came over to us and showed me they had information for humans about horses' feet. I showed them I would listen and write down what they sent me.

Hard devices - humans place - our feet - confine our feet. Moons - seasons - we accepted - hard devices. Hard devices - important - of humans.	moons = months seasons = years
We agreed - service of humans. We no know - many seasons cycles - hard devices - disrupting - our body rhythms. Creating - body disturbance - of balance.	For a long time horses accepted wearing shoes, unaware of the disruptive effect.
Life - movement. Movement ways of doing - worked - hard devices - collection moons - seasons cycles. Ways of doing serve - purpose - many seasons cycles. Purpose - served - seasons cycles movement - evolves/creates - new purpose - way of doing.	The use of metal shoes worked for a long time.

Beginning - change of movement - purpose - way of doing - hard devices - humans place our feet.

Through their use evolved a new way of thinking; horses no longer wearing shoes.

We are beginning to change our management of horses' feet.

Season - expansion - of knowing - humans - us combined.

expansion of knowing = consciousness

We continue service - giving humans - use our bodies. Us - know discomfort feet - we accept way of being. We ask - humans - grow aware - discomfort our feet - old purpose - way of doing. We ask - new purpose - way of doing. Relieving - our discomfort - our feet.

The idea of barefoot.

We now - seasons cycle - creating purpose - way of doing - allowing - us freedom - discomfort - our feet.

Why humans - resist - new purpose - way of doing? Why humans - find - new purpose - way of doing - challenging? Why humans - cling? Why humans - fear new ways?

new purpose = barefoot

New way doing - solve problems - both - humans - us. Our feet functioning - no discomfort - allow us - move - human jobs - freer movement body.

Humans - like better movement - of our bodies? Better movement - our bodies create - pleasing of humans?

We wear - hard devices - our feet - touch earth - jarring us. Sharp motion - moves up - our legs - our shoulder - hips. Over seasons - our bodies - move less - freely. We want - move freely.

Less freedom - movement - over seasons cycle - creates frustration of us. No good way - feel of us. We enjoy - ease movement - calm inner way.

We want - humans - know - we feel - freer movement - our bodies - no hard devices - our feet. We ask - humans - create - soft device our feet.	soft device = sport shoes like humans wear
We ask - no hard device - our feet - touch earth - rhythm balanced. Feet touch earth - no hard device - feet expand - rhythm of movement - our body. No sharp - jar. Contact - impact - moves freely - up our legs. Our bodies - softer - fluid. We like. Less discomfort - our bodies - movement body - flowing. Pleasing picture - us - humans.	
Humans of power - please look inside - new purpose - way of doing.	humans of power = owner
We ask - humans.	

The pictures stopped, and I sat quietly. My friends waited for me to speak. I read them what their horses showed me. We were in awe of the clarity of their message. This was not the first time I had heard this information from horses. It had come up before with horses who were having foot problems.

I had received the picture of sport shoes or sneakers for horses before—this time it was even clearer. They wanted devices on their feet that were as comfortable as sports shoes are for humans. This is an image they get from our minds. It was, however, the first time I had written down the horses' views on shoeing, and it led to this chapter.

Dom, Faustina, Gus, Larry, Ponce, Safire, Starbuck, Sunshower

Dom - Lusitano/Thoroughbred gelding. Gray. 3½ years old.

Faustina - Thoroughbred mare. Bay. 14 years old.

Ponce - Andalusian/Thoroughbred gelding. Gray. 4½ years old.

Starbuck - Appaloosa gelding. Black. 3 years old.

Sunshower - Quarter Horse mare. Palomino. 9 years old.

October 25, 2004

This had been a tough day at the hospital with my Dad. It was clear he was dying. Once more, I went to Barbara's farm to be with her horses. I went into the pasture and was surrounded. The horses crowded around me, nuzzling me softly. They felt my sadness and did their best to help me feel better.

Amy came to the fence, and the horses started sending—they had more to show us about shoes. We walked over and sat on the big bale of hay in the shed, ready to hear what the horses had to share.

We ask - show our feet.	
Humans in care of us - hard devices off our feet.	Humans who care for us took our shoes off.
Young human mare - shown - no hard devices our feet. Young human mares - tools of hand using - small. Young human mare - softly - works our feet - allowing us alignment of bone. Alignment - allow us - freedom - movement of body. Our feet - contact earth - flowing rhythm of motion.	Another human taught Amy how to care for their feet without shoes.
Young mare human - soft yet - firm of us.	

We enjoy young human mares - treatment - our feet. We freer movement - our bodies now. We hard devices on our feet - our bodies - discomfort. We moved - our movement - more - effort of us. Difficult seasons of cycle of us.	Difficult over long period of time.
We ask humans - hear us. We ask humans - consider - way our feet cared of. We ask humans - see season cycle - exciting opportunity creating solutions - our feet - rhythm movement flowing.	
We ask humans - see season of creating - flowing movement. We ask humans - no be afraid - new purpose - of way of doing.	
We feel - easier in our bodies. Please hear us.	

Again, I read to Amy what the horses had shown me. It was a lovely confirmation for her natural hoof care work. Moving away from the established method was not easy. We asked ourselves if we were really doing the right thing when a large portion of the population saw things differently.

As the horses saw it, movement was harder with shoes on. Their bodies moved more freely, and they were more comfortable without shoes.

Gus, Ponce, Safire

October 28, 2004

I was again at Barbara's farm getting a horse fix. My world was moving toward a huge change as my Dad was barely hanging on. I was very grateful to come here and have quiet time with the horses. I appreciated having time to recharge myself, time to reflect and time to accept. The horses approached me again. Amy was there and sat with me on the big hay bale. It was a cozy, sunny and pleasant spot.

Change - rapidly moving - combined human - horse world.

Change is happening for both humans and horses.

Old way doing - served - many - many - cycles of seasons. We - no blame - humans way - doing of past. Ways of doing - evolve - need of function. Need of function - dictates - way of doing - series season of cycles. Function - steady - series season cycles.

The "old ways" stayed that way for a long time.

Movement evolve - tiny tiny movement - long series seasons cycles. Movement evolve - gathers momentum. We now - seasons cycles - momentum gathering - creation - way of doing unfolds. Creating ways of doing - allowing our bodies - function of movement - alignment our bodies - truly move.

Universal raising of the collective consciousness.

Humans mind - enjoy complicated - creations. Make humans - feel smart. Humans need - feel smart - over us. Why humans - need feel - this way? Is simple - creation - no enough? Is not being with us - simply enough?

Our feet - bodies sore - with hard devices.

We ask humans - use collected momentum - evolving - no hard devices our feet.

We want continue - humans created jobs - we do of humans. We ask - allowed do human created job - our bodies - feet flow easily - no soreness.

Possible now. Answers - not in humans mind. Answer - in humans heart - of seeing.

Humans - learn see - heart seeing. Simple. Mind - rigid - complicated. We nudge humans daily - humans work with us.

No sore feet - bodies allow joyful movement - between humans - us.

Hear us.

Amy and I were speechless after I read aloud what the horses shared. We sat watching them in awe of their generosity and wisdom.

I left and drove back to the hospital. While driving, I felt peaceful—ready to face what lay ahead with my Dad. Unknown to me then, my Dad would die within the next 24 hours.

Brutus

Quarter Horse gelding. Chestnut, narrow blaze. 6 years old.

January 20, 2005

I was in Virginia visiting my friend Joe, a brilliant professional horseman. His work with the horses in his care was clear and kind. The horses had an opportunity to learn in a relaxed, safe environment, and Joe was a joy to watch when working with a horse. The horses adored him.

Brutus was in cross-ties in the grooming area of the barn where Joe was working. A farrier was trying to shoe him, and it was not going well. Brutus was fidgety, and the farrier was doing his best to not lose his temper. Joe had moved to this young horse's head to try to soothe him. Brutus started to settle down.

I began to get pictures and grabbed my notebook to start writing.

Why humans no hear - we call distress - humans placing - hard devices - our feet. We call - human stop.

Hard devices our feet - no fully touch earth. Blood no flows - properly - our feet. Our heels rigid - no moving in - out.

Some us - no feel our feet. We separate - our feet - our awareness - continue - serve our jobs.

They block feeling to their feet so they are able to continue service to a human.

Our feet cramped - hard devices. Hard devices - created - no resonate - our innate - beingness. Our beingness - soft movement - all directions. Our feet - movement - all directions. Hard devices - no allow - all direction movement. Hard devices - contains movement - forcing movement - up leg bones - move. Bones move - no meant carry - forced movement up leg. We shut down - we continue do job - of humans. We want do job.

Joints have unbalanced movement.

Movement seasons cycles - many many - we silently - carry - hard devices our feet. We accepted hard devices - humans thought - we needed do our job.

We bow - to humans.

We waking up - humans waking up. We evolve - see we do our jobs - no hard devices.

Both horses and humans begin to see they can do their jobs with no shoes.

We grateful mare human - who hears us. Helps know - our calls heard. Calls heard - humans use creative nature - change humans treatment our feet.

mare human = author

Collective consciousness humans - us - expands - evolves - now season cycle movement.

There is a collective consciousness growing now for horses and humans alike.

Humans hearing us - creating softer ways - handling our feet - humans heart hearing. Humans mind - no creativity - no answers - no hearing.

Mind - only hear mind.

Humans listening hearts - our work together - becomes movement - flowing effortlessly between humans - us. Creating deeper partnership - of both.

I had not looked at these handwritten notes since they were written over a year ago. As I typed them into my computer, I was struck by the common thread that ran through what the horses in New York showed me, and what this young horse in Virginia showed me three months later.

Jossett

Dutch Warmblood mare. Bay. 14 years old.

April 8, 2005

I was back in New York at Barbara's farm. Amy was doing natural hoof care work on Jossett. This mare's job had been dressage, but she was no longer able to work due to lameness. She was very sweet, sensitive and willing.

My being there was not planned; it simply worked out that I was on the East Coast when this mare arrived. We decided I could listen to Jossett while Amy pulled her shoes and gave Jossett her first natural hoof care trim.

It was wonderful to work that way. If I translate while a horse is being worked on, I get immediate feedback from the horse and can share what they are feeling with the human working with them.

I willing. Young human mare - taking hard devices.	
I no feel my feet - always. I discomfort hind end. Feet numb.	Most of the time.

Jossett showed me that the atrophy in her body was due to feet that were out of balance. She showed me that the clips on the shoes created a dead area with pressure points she could not escape. As Amy pulled the left-hind shoe, Jossett told me her foot tingled. As the foot touched the ground, a shock sensation rushed up the entire inside of her leg. She was flooded with the release of the foot trauma and the emotional relief of having the shoe off.

My level of service - willingness - overrides discomfort. I tune - discomfort out.

For a long time, Jossett had been tuning out her discomfort. Many horses do this. Now she no longer had to. Jossett sent a picture of the heat in her left hip as it opened up from increased blood flow. She also pointed out that the rasping of the left hind hoof was soothing.

Soon another huge emotional release happened. Waves of worry and grief at being unable to do her job were leaving her body. This was an accumulation from the damage to her body from wearing shoes for many years. Amy next pulled the front shoes. It was also a relief when they came off.

At this point, Jossett could not stand on her left hind leg in order to work on the right hind foot. I worked with her gently, stepping each foot forward and back, left and right. By moving her body slowly in different directions, she was able to release both physical and emotional tension. Jossett soon began to lick and chew. Her eyes got much softer, and she was able to relax. Then Jossett was able to lift her right hind foot for Amy.

My power human - moves outside - humans know box - helpful of me.

Why humans - no see - affects doing - result us feeling effects of doing.

Humans - shut down.

Jossett's owner was operating outside her range of knowledge, but was willing to explore unknown territory to help her horse.

Why don't humans see the effects of wearing metal shoes on horses' bodies?

As Jossett put her foot down after a shoe came off, the release of foot trauma sent tingling sensations up her legs in waves, and awareness came back in each foot. Had I not known what she felt, I would have taken how she moved for soreness and would have thought she needed to have the shoes back on.

Jossett showed us she was willing to be in discomfort as her body repaired itself. The mending would be a slow process and one that she would willingly participate in. She was orally given homeopathic remedies to help her with the stress and shock going on in her system. Her body began the business of repairing her feet and balancing itself. Our job was to support Jossett and not try to fix, stop or take away the discomfort we saw as pain.

Jossett was hand walked to stimulate her body's repair response. Each day, the soreness lessened as her body grew new sole and new healthy hoof wall. All of this was done with the help of a veterinarian, who managed Jossett's homeopathic care. It was amazing how fast her body repaired itself when she was given a chance to exist and move in a way that worked for her body.

In a couple of weeks, her owner was riding Jossett in the outdoor arena for short periods. After seven weeks, she was walking in the hay fields, slowly building her body back to a balanced whole.

The entire process was slow. There was no instant, miracle cure. Jossett understood that temporary discomfort would create a response from her body to repair itself. The outcome was that after years of being lame and uncomfortable in her body, Jossett was sound.

Jossett was a willing teacher. She and the other horses were helping us move in a new direction of managing horses' feet. Our horses have much to show us, if we will listen to them.

Star Chaser

Warmblood gelding. Gray.

January 14, 2006

My friend Dan was a farrier, and included natural hoof care in his work. He called me about a horse I had also worked with recently. As I was checking in with this horse, another horse named Star Chaser, a jumper, wanted to show me his feet. Dan was excited to hear his feedback, as Star Chaser was also his client.

Star Chaser showed me what it felt like to jump and land with an unbalanced, shod hoof. The following describes the path of the shock of landing traveling up his front leg into the shoulder and withers.

Coffin bone - jams toe.

To heel - to front of pastern.

To back of fetlock.

To front cannon.

To back of knee.

To front forearm.

To back side elbow.

To front point shoulder.

To top shoulder at wither.

Jams the withers - compresses the withers.

The next piece describes what Star Chaser felt when landing after a jump with a balanced hoof.

Balanced - wholeness - aliveness - hoof structure. Shock - trauma follows a different route.

Shock landing - distributed - evenly - through sole.

Bottom side - coffin bone - shock evenly - dispersed.

Shock travels up through center of leg evenly all the way up.

Shock absorbed through whole shoulder.

Shock has been evenly distributed all the way up - less trauma to all leg structures.

Feels better of me.

As Star Chaser showed me the route of shock trauma, I could literally feel it as it traveled up his leg. It is a very powerful insight into how it feels for horses jumping on feet that are out of balance.

CONSIDERATIONS

The beginning parts of this chapter came to me as I went through the death of my Dad. Being with Barbara's and Amy's horses during that time was a much-needed gift.

As the horses have shared with me, the consciousness of humans and horses alike are expanding. We are looking at ways that will serve horses by helping them to be more comfortable as they perform their jobs for us. They are asking to go barefoot so their bodies can function well and stay in balance. The barefoot approach is controversial. Assimilating new approaches into the established way of doing things will take time. It is an evolution.

Having a horse go barefoot may be a problem, for example, when their shoes are pulled after many years of wearing them. Some of the horses I've worked with were asking for a type of sport shoe or sneaker that supports the hoof as it comes back into balance. Devices now on the market move in this direction but do not offer the flexibility the horses are asking for. The technology is there—we simply need to continue to look outside the box and create.

A book devoted solely to horses' feet is next. I am already collecting amazing information and images from horses. They are taking me into more detailed, deeper levels of hoof function.

Chapter 6

Old Horses

I am blessed by the many old horses I have known over the years. Some of them were my teachers when I was a child, and some were school horses that helped me to teach beginner children and adults. They had a gentle, kind and sometimes-opinionated way about them.

I remember a lovely old pony named Paris who I used for children learning to ride a canter. Paris knew and liked her job.

In one lesson I was teaching a child named Anna to canter on Paris. I explained to Anna the proper use of her legs while keeping her hands "quiet." Anna looked at me, and with the supreme confidence of a six year old, told me all *she* had to do was tell Paris, "canter, canter" and Paris would canter. I emphasized to Anna using her legs was the proper way to have Paris canter.

Without missing a beat, Anna said, "Paris, canter, canter!" and Paris immediately went into her slow, easy canter. Anna was beaming and told her riding instructor, "See, I told you so!" I was handed another dose of humility while the two of them happily cantered around the ring. Paris threw me a look too, and with a gleam in her eye that also said, "I told you so!"

Elderly horses with thoughts to express are speaking from years of wisdom they want to share with humans. Their way of being touches my heart.

Pokey

Quarter Horse gelding. Bay, no markings. 30 years old.

August 21, 2004

We met Pokey in the chapter on death and dying. He is the only horse to appear twice in this book. He and I had a very close connection because the shed in his pen shared a wall with my apartment. We could look at each other through a window in that shared wall, making it nice for both of us. I enjoyed his company, and I could not take myself *too* seriously when I looked into his wise, old face.

Pokey came to the window and gave me the horse look that says, "I have something to show you." His eyes were bright and he felt cheerful to me. I got my folding chair and notebook and went outside to the fence. Pokey wanted to tell me about old horses.

Cycles seasons - my body old. Life - pleasing of me. Living place - of me - cycles seasons. Humans changed - stay of me. Care of me - soft. Food plenty.	The humans changed but he stayed.
Humans - see me - now space. Humans - sad hearts. Humans - no understand - cycles seasons of body.	Humans sad to see my old body.
My body - holds less flesh now. Human ways - no good look - of me.	He is very thin.
Horse ways - life cycle - no sad - cycles seasons. My body - slowing - making flesh harder. I no feel bad. I content with friends. I special roaming space - graze.	Not sad to be old. He is allowed to roam around the barns, which he likes.
Humans - take our lives - we no ready leave our bodies.	Sometimes older horses are put down before they are ready to go.

Cycles seasons old body of us - no able do job. Some us miss our job. Some us content no job. Be horse - do horse way - good way being.

We cycles seasons body horses - ask humans - listen to us. We show humans - we ready leave body of us. No assume - we looking less flesh - we feeling unbalanced rhythm of body. Individual each of us - rhythm our leaving.

feeling unbalanced rhythm of body = ill

My worry - I made leave - no ready leave. Hard convince humans - we fine - we less flesh.

We see life - is experience. Being less flesh - cycles seasons old body - experience of us. Being discomfort - experience of us. Humans labels of unbalance of body - no meaning of us. Our bodies - many expressions of being. We no live - avoid - discomfort. Discomfort - experience living - in a body. Humans look of us - assume we same - seeing life - as humans do. Humans place - humans view life - upon us - seeing cycles seasons horse - less flesh.

human labels of unbalance of body = diseases

Pain and illness are part of life cycle.

Humans see - cycles seasons horse less flesh - humans sad. Humans - think - do something. I cycles seasons horse - less flesh - I enjoy each sun. Sun feels good my back. I eat my fill. I walk - where pleases me. I content no job.

each sun = day

Humans see body - no perfect - no life. We see body - no perfect - experience life = perfect.

We ask humans - see us - individuals - listen - our wanting. Listen to us - see richer way - living.

My human - good job - doing of me. I content - cycles season body - less flesh.

Pokey helped me see things from a different point of view. Instead of feeling sadness when I saw his physical body, I now saw a great old horse having the time of his life. He would let us know when he was ready to leave his body. Pokey was giving us the same message as in the chapter on death and dying, that discomfort was the experience of living in a body.

March 29, 2005

I was leaving for the East Coast for the month of April. I went to Pokey's pen at dawn, right outside my front door. I wanted to see him before I left, as I knew he was getting close to leaving. He was standing by the fence, looking at me. That look let me know he would not be there when I returned. We shared a lovely last moment, and I thanked him for what he had shown me about the horse's way of being old.

I felt sad and was in tears. He gave me a nudge with his head and clearly sent me the message that he was fine. He showed me that going was no big deal. For him, it was simply a part of life. He was very old and his body was wearing out—it was that simple.

Pokey died the week before I came home. The pen seemed empty without him, even though there were two elderly llamas and an old mare in that space. By July 1st, these three would be gone, too. I miss seeing their old faces. Life is coming and going. I don't have to hold on like I used to.

The last week of May a sturdy colt was born—a new life beginning after Pokey's going. I am beginning to see life in the rhythms the horses show me.

Commander

Stallion. Brown, no markings. 25 years old.

I was asked to work with Commander, an elderly stallion with popular bloodlines. He was having problems in the breeding shed when being collected. The people working with him asked me if I would get his point of view on what was going wrong so they could understand and help.

I headed to his stall and asked for Commander's permission to work with him. He readily agreed.

May 3, 2005

I very tired. My hind legs - grow weak. Rising up - hard.	Mounting the phantom in the breeding shed is getting hard.
I with human - work. Human - ask me work. I try.	For the handler in breeding shed, he tries.
I want stop breeding. I want be - horse now. No job.	
Humans control of me - no understand. Humans ask - more more.	humans control of me = his owners
My seed - no create strong foals. Foals created now - vital spark less. Simple way - life body seasons. Body seasons slower.	body seasons slower = old body
I want stay here. Be voice to humans - control of me.	He wants to stay in the place were the handler is, as he likes this person and trusts him. He has asked the handler to be his voice with his owners.
I - best body able do job asked.	He will do his best till the end of the breeding season. Then he wants to retire and stay at this place, which he really likes, and just be a horse.
Balances - my body changing. Simply is. My body - pushed long seasons.	

Balance - do job now. Balance - stay in body.

It is a delicate balance how much longer he can do his job and how much longer he will be alive in his body.

For the rest of the breeding season, I worked with Commander and his handler. Commander kept expressing how tired he was, and that he was doing his best to meet the wishes of the handler, who was trying very hard to work with this stallion in a respectful way.

The owners' views were quite different. They did not believe that horses could "talk"—they were just animals, not sentient beings. Their stallion had a job to do, regardless of the circumstances. The owners had many bookings for him that they wanted completed. Commander was a big moneymaker for them.

Toward the end of the breeding season, he was no longer able to breed. Commander showed me his body was too tired. A couple of months after the season ended, he was found in his stall with colic. The colic was very serious, and he died before surgery could be performed. The necropsy revealed his large colon had ruptured. Commander had clearly told me his body was slowing down and had reached the point of not being able to breed. His owners were unable or unwilling to grasp he was slowing down, and that he wanted to retire and be a horse.

CONSIDERATIONS

Oftentimes the human expectation of old horses is beyond what the horses' bodies can handle. Horses are so willing to perform their jobs that they will do so to their own detriment. We, as owners of and companions to these animals, need to respect and allow horses to function at a level that is best for *them* at any given time in their lives. The horses are giving us a wonderful gift of wisdom about the rhythms of life—we are the ones who have much to learn in this area, if we will only listen.

Once again, these were the horses who drew me to them. Pokey's and Commander's messages are what is important to the horses at this time. They would like us to pay attention to their inner wisdom and rhythms.

Chapter 7

Alternative Healing Methods

There are many alternative healing methods for horses, including acupuncture, homeopathy, massage, magnets and chiropractic. Practitioners have varying levels of expertise, ranging from skilled veterinarians using complementary medicines and procedures in their practices, to people who read a book and start using a technique or remedy on their own animals.

Based on the billions of dollars spent annually, the public generally views alternative healing methods and products favorably. They are looking for answers. However, this area is not without controversy and skeptics regarding practices with both humans and animals. Results may be excellent in some situations and not with others.

My own introduction into alternative health care came in 1988 when I began studying Jin Shin Jyutsu, an ancient art of balancing the body's energy by applying light pressure to specific safety energy locks. The training brought me inside the world of complementary care and in contact with a veterinarian who used homeopathy, craniosacral therapy and chiropractic in her practice. My experiences with this vet and the animals in her care, along with my Jin Shin Jyutsu knowledge, helped me translate the horses' messages on this topic. It enabled me to clearly hear what felt good and what did not to animals receiving alternative care.

For the most part, the horses in this chapter preferred not to be identified, so there are sections with no names or descriptions. Reading the following chapter may be an eye opener—it certainly was for me as I listened to the horses' point of view.

Various Horses as a Collective

August 30, 2004

The following came from several horses shortly after they had had some form of alternative care. The feedback was, at times, surprising. Sometimes, what a horse felt did not match what the human was telling me about their perception of how the horse was feeling. This was another opportunity for me to trust myself when I was being shown something by the horses that ran counter to what humans were expressing.

Our bodies - unfairly touched. Some us - submit. Submitting - way of life - many of us.	
We no know - humans systems.	human systems = reiki, acupuncture, homeopathy, magnets, essential oils, electronic machines, lasers, massage therapy, etc.
Act our submitting - no mean we give permission. Permission - submitting - separate of us	
Why humans - place hands - humans pushing devices - on our bodies - no asking - we want humans hands - humans pushing devices on us?	humans pushing devices = machines
Why humans - no see us - beings of own feelings?	
Humans systems - no permission given of us - intrusive of us. Creating unbalance movement - inside us. Why humans think - humans right of force - our bodies repair? Forcing repair - allowing our bodies continue move humans jobs - base of force - repair of us. Human desire of our bodies - move humans ways - base repair of us.	Humans forcing our bodies to heal, so horses can continue to perform their jobs.
Humans think - our service of humans - humans right of us. Humans forget - agreement of us - service of humans.	Humans think it is their right to use horses.

We ask humans - look deeply - humans actions - attitude - placing humans hands - humans pushing devices - substances on - in our bodies.	substances = oils, herbs, homeopathic remedies, magnets, machines, etc.
Why humans - reason of action? Humans thought - truly benefit us? Humans asking us - our want of our body? Humans listening - our response - if we asked? Why humans - no ask us - we feel of us?	Ask what we want.
Emotions - horse way.	Their emotions are simpler than human emotions, yet powerful in their simplicity.
Humans systems - go our emotion place - intrusive - invading us - no our openness - work emotion place inside us. Damage our sensitive systems - we unconsciously invaded of humans.	no our openness = not our permission Humans unconsciously invade us.
Human attitude - fixing - felt of us - both divisions repair.	They show me both alternative healing methods and conventional veterinary medicine.
Humans pushing devices - disks - push our bodies - repair. Harsh - our body systems. Repair - surface level. Felt - force - our bodies. Pushing our bodies - against movement of our bodies internal movement of balance.	disks = magnets
Humans - no awareness - use machines - disks - disruptive of us. Humans - awareness use - in flow of us - use smaller disruptive.	Machines and magnets used by humans in a more aware state are less, yet still, disruptive.
We function flawed. Our view - humans unnatural expectation - perfect movement our bodies. We ask - all human bodies move perfect body movement? We ask - human kicked out - living box no move perfect body movement?	Are humans forced to leave their homes because they do not move perfectly? Horses are sold, forced to leave home, because some of them don't move the way humans think they should.

How our bodies move - human jobs - no always proper perspective - how we move. Humans thought - use humans systems - force our body movement. Human systems - assure our movement - equal human thought - standard our movement.

Humans create standards how horses should move.

Why humans - no see - simplicity our movement? Why our movement demanded - more more - better better? Why more - better - do of who we are. Confusing of us.

Why is who we are not enough for humans?

Our bodies developed - flee predators. Our true function.

We no refuse. We ask humans - respect use of us. When humans disrespect - our bodies - humans disrespect humans. We ask humans - slow down - see - hear us.

Humans do the same disrespect to other humans.

Use human systems - speed body repair response. Humans no like - wait life unfolding. Life unfolding - repair body - slow movement of us - horse way. Muscle pulled far - torn - human want fix fast. Why humans - demand life move fast? Repair fast? Why important of humans?

Humans want faster healing of horses' bodies.

Humans demand - much our bodies use - repair.

It was a demanding session with these horses. Translating their images was, at times, slow as I struggled for accuracy. It was important to horses that we understood that using machines, magnets and other modalities could be harsh on their systems. They showed me a picture of a horse standing quietly while being worked on, with the humans thinking the horse was doing well. Instead, the horse was going deep inside to escape the disturbance of the machine treatment.

I was also shown how "giving permission" looked. The horse's eyes are bright; he is willing to stand quietly; and he shows interest and curiosity about what the person is doing to him. The horse will be licking and chewing and have a relaxed body. Not all these indicators may be present at the same time.

Next I was shown how "submitting" looked. The horse's eyes are dull or worried and often looking inward. His body is tense, sometimes sweating, back hollowed, breathing shallow and tail clamped. He could be wiggling and trying to walk away. Again, not all these negative indicators may be exhibited at the same time.

The horses are asking us to look at what we are doing. They are telling us that just because we think these machines, products or procedures are the latest new technology or "natural," it does not mean they are the best things for the horses. We are being asked to use all alternative care with greater awareness. Over and over horses show me their systems are much more sensitive than ours. Less is better as their systems are easily over-loaded.

The next part of the message was about why humans push horses' bodies to repair so fast after they sustain injuries doing the jobs we created. They show us their bodies have a slower repair pace or movement. Why are humans in such a hurry?

Horses are asking us to slow down and listen so they can show us what works. There is a lot to digest in this piece.

September 1, 2004

The horses had more to show me.

Why humans fear - slow down. Moving fast - no see life - no hear life. Humans hearing us - humans mind slow.

Repairing - is rhythm. Rhythm - own movement. Each horse body - own rhythm movement of repairing. Rhythm - individual each horse. Slow - fast - many factors of horse - depth injury - level of beingness - emotional place wanting repair - surroundings - life journey lessons of horse. Factors of human -

To hear them, our minds must be quiet. In my experience, if my mind is busy, I don't hear the horses—I only hear me.

level of beingness = health

emotional place wanting repair = attitude

surroundings = stall bound or turned out

humans attitude of fixing - emotions level - level consciousness - knowledge level of human method - level allowing life rhythm. Affects - repairing unfolding.

emotions level = fear, anger, peaceful, calm

level consciousness = autopilot, present, or aware

level allowing life rhythm = the level at which the human allows life's rhythm of unfolding

Many methods of humans. Humans often - asleep of true nature of methods.

How well does the human understand the modality being used? There are many levels of understanding.

Humans seeing - of repairing - want no mess. Clean - tidy - pleasant - fast. Nature of repairing - messy - discomfort - up down emotions - soft - sharp movement.

No formula. Individual - horse individual. Plus - horse - human mixture - working together.

Life horse body - movement all directions - levels rhythm - each horse being.

Is movement - humans want control. We see movement - freely. Humans see movement - humans dictate.

No fixing. Repairing - is no direction aimed. Fixing - is direction aimed. Repairing - unfolds movement. Fixing - limits movement. Repairing - is effortless. Fixing - is work.

We ask humans - before humans place - humans hands - humans pushing devices - disks - substances on us - in us - ask our permission. Be quiet with us. Hear us. Be in flow with us.

Humans be with us - respectfully of us - open wonderful unfolding.

We ask humans - be of us - feeling - seeing - hearing. Mind - slow - calm - open.

Quiet soft union with us - humans come home - humans inner being.

Our gift - to humans.

This piece was huge. It opened the door to make me really take a look at the place I was in when I cared for a horse who had a wound or injury. Was I on autopilot doing what I was taught, or did I stop and listen? I was learning about awareness, being conscious and being present in the moment. There are many levels of consciousness. I am beginning to see that when I learn one level, then the next one opens up. It is a constant flow taking me deeper into the horses' and my own being. The more the horses show me, the more I learn about life.

There is a spiritual essence to this chapter. I did not purposely go in that direction. It was simply part of the flow. Allowing myself to go where I am led takes me to amazing experiences. With these experiences, I expand how I view life—not just how I view the horses, but all life.

This book is a journey, not a destination. Every time I arrive at a destination, I realize it is a resting place and not the end of the journey. The momentum slows almost to a halt, giving me a chance to digest, and then the momentum picks up again. I could exchange the word "movement" for momentum.

Mimi

Quarter Horse mare. Black, blaze, two hind socks.
10 years old.

April 11, 2006

Almost a year-and-a-half would go by before I was given more information for this chapter. I thought it was done. The horses did not share my point of view. Mimi made it very clear she had things to say. She blasted into my head demanding I pay attention to her.

Mimi, with her permission, was receiving constitutional homeopathy from a veterinarian with training as a homeopath. The homeopathic remedy was working deep in her body, and as a result, Mimi was forming a large abscess in her left front foot, preparing to release toxins.

Her owner, Jessica, asked me to check with Mimi to see how she was feeling, and she began showing me what was happening in her body. Mimi clearly showed me her body's inner movement, which I labeled "healing." Mimi immediately came back with "healing" is a human concept and that horses see life as movement. For them, everything is movement and the rhythm of movement. Mimi did not suffer fools lightly.

We asked Mimi if she would work with me so I could share her view with humans. She agreed. The images were complicated, so translating was slow. Mimi made it very clear how important it was for humans to hear the horses' point of view on this concept of "healing."

No our perspective - healing. Healing - human perspective.

Horses - no concept healing.

Horses see - movements of our inner body - creating wholeness for survival.

Our bodies - inner knowing of movement - creating balance of body functions. Balance of body functions - creates ability - us physically move in our environment - for survival. Our dance with humans - changes inner movements. Survival in human care - less movement both inner and outer.

In wild living - our inner movements - full expression.

Human living of us - our inner movements interrupted by human effects on us. We willingly live - human place of living. Willing participation.

human effects = vaccines, diet, work, medications, small living space, blankets, etc.

Jessica and I wanted more explanation. Mimi sent me pictures of how humans have to examine and pick at something until it is barely recognizable, and she called us on it. Mimi couldn't understand what possessed humans to think they could rule the earth. I felt humbled.

We simply do. No repeating. It simply is.

Humans make big deal - our bodies repairing. Humans fixed idea - repairing is. Humans push - manipulate bodies - humans - ours - conform humans image of healing. We no concept - humans view.

Our view - movement - inner - outer.

Jessica asked if it was okay to voice more questions for Mimi.

I may no answer.

Mimi was getting agitated. From her point of view, she was making things very clear to us. Then Jessica asked if this was a summation of Mimi's entire experience.

It simply is movement. Living horse body - is movement. Birth is movement. Death is movement. Discomfort is movement. Sound is movement. Feeling is movement. Touch is movement. Eating is movement. Our beingness is movement.

Humans forget - movement. Humans create barriers - push movement - into small segmented boxes - where movement loses flow.

small segmented boxes = over analyzing

Next Jessica asked if movement, like everything, is made of energy vibration.

Energy vibration - human concept.

Life is movement

Mimi was done. She had shown me what she wanted and was not interested in repeating herself. Mimi was agitated, and clearly it was not her fault. To her, the questions we were asking were not necessary. "What part of 'life is movement' don't humans get?" was basically Mimi's message.

Humans label things horses don't. The word "movement" was the closest word I found to match what Mimi and other horses have shown about how they see life in a horses' body and how it is for them to repair their bodies.

Mimi's experience with homeopathy was good. The abscess was the result of her body working to balance itself. She made it clear she had discomfort, but she was fine. She was very lame and kept showing Jessica and me, "Don't worry what it looks like, I am doing okay." This was really helpful to Jessica; otherwise, she would have done the typical human thing and worried. Working this way created clarity for both sides. I realized how straightforward and simple horses were—no complicated analyzing, picking things apart or having to go around and around. Horses show me things, and I translate it into English. It is that simple. What humans do with the information is up to them.

Five days after I worked with Mimi on this piece, the abscess ruptured. Mimi lost the sole of her hoof from behind the point of the frog all the way to the toe. It looked terrible, but Mimi told us not to worry. Immediately, her body began to grow new sole. In forty-eight hours, she was sound. Mimi demonstrated to us what a horse's body looks like when it is allowed to balance itself within its own inner rhythms.

CONSIDERATIONS

What the horses showed me in this chapter is that alternative healing methods are not used with knowledge, integrity, respect and permission. Basically, the horses show me all the time that humans do not take the time to stop and consider what the horse wants. This is also true of traditional medicine for horses.

People seem to think because something is natural or alternative that it can cause no harm, and if a little is good, then more is better. As a trained practitioner of Jin Shin Jyutsu, I learned immediately that a horse's energy systems are different than humans. In my experience, horses become overloaded if we try to do the same amount of work with them as we would do with a human.

I learned this the hard way. On my first time using Jin Shin Jyutsu on a horse, I was enthusiastic and wanted to do a good job with the horse. I worked for a while, and he began to shift, but I did not pay attention. He moved out from under my hands, and I still did not pay attention. The next thing I knew, I was flying across the wash stall and hit the wall because he had kicked me there. I picked myself up, looked at him and said, "I get it. You have had enough." After that, I paid attention and always stopped when a horse showed me that he had had enough.

Horses have been very clear with me about how they feel after treatment with various alternative healing methods. More times than you might think, they did not feel good. One reason the horses did not feel good was that their energy was changing and moving in their bodies. Coming back into balance is not a straight line. Things may get worse before they get better. It takes time to get out of balance, and it takes time to reestablish balance.

The second reason for a horse not to feel good is there is too much treatment. Humans assume because horses have larger bodies, there is a need to use more of a product or to treat for a longer period of time. Not true; with horses—*less is better!*

The horses are giving us a heads up. They are asking us to be conscious of what we are doing. They are asking us to be conscious of how powerful these modalities are on their sensitive systems and to use them carefully and respectfully.

I am blessed to have a friend who is a veterinarian who uses homeopathy, chiropractic, craniosacral and nutritional counseling in her practice. Over the last eight years, I have worked with a number of her clients. I've learned much about how a horse's body responds to homeopathy, craniosacral, chiropractic and nutrition to help repair itself. I now recognize that when these modalities work well for a horse, it is because the treatment is balanced.

A horse's response to "balanced" work has a very different feel than the response caused by too much work. In both instances, the horse may not feel well, but his attitude is different.

To sum it up, we have wonderful new tools to use. We simply need to use them with knowledge, integrity, respect and permission. That might mean not to use them at all. The most important piece to remember is to listen and observe when horses have had enough. The last thing our horses need is for us to be like a bunch of five-year-olds with loaded guns.

The horses' graciousness and generosity in giving us this information is not about making humans wrong. They are simply showing us that their systems are different from ours.

Chapter 8

Wild Horses

Being from the East Coast, I had no contact or experience with wild horses until I moved to New Mexico in 1999. A woman soon asked me to halter-break three wild horses. She had bought a two-year-old stallion and a four-year-old mare at auction. The mare's filly, born at this woman's small farm, was one month old.

The first time I walked into the pen with these horses, the mare pinned her ears flat and clearly let me know I was not to come any closer. I stood quietly and waited. She was angry to be away from her herd in this confined place. No one had asked her if she had wanted to come here. The mare wanted me to take the three of them back to the wild. I had to show her I did not have the power to do so.

Working with them, I quickly realized these horses were different than the domestic horses I had worked with on the East Coast. Their wild nature was much closer to the surface. I found myself rethinking how I worked. I learned a great deal from these wild horses. It pushed me to expand my work with horses in general.

A few years later, I had the privilege of visiting wild horse herds in New Mexico and Colorado through Judy, a woman I met through a mutual friend. She was a wild horse photographer and round-up volunteer in the El Rito Ranger District. The images I gathered from the wild horses while I sat and listened to their point of view held surprises. They took me on a special and educational journey.

The subject of wild horses is an emotional one, no matter what your personal position on their management might be. For us Easterners especially, wild horses are a symbol of wide-open spaces, of freedom and of the West. Read this chapter with an open mind and heart. The messages given by these wild horses are powerful and thought provoking.

Esparanza

Wild horse mare. Bay. 30-35 years old.

August 26, 2004

Judy called to ask if I could connect with an older, pregnant lead mare that had been taken to a holding area. The U.S. Forest Service culled this mare and several other horses from the El Rito Ranger District.

The Forest Service rangers were going to release a young stallion back into the area from which this group of horses were taken. Judy tried to have the older lead mare released with the young stallion, thought to be her son. The Forest Service decided against it and released the stallion on his own.

Judy was able to adopt the mare, now named Esparanza, and took her and two other mares from Esparanza's herd to a friend's ranch. Even though she was with two mares she knew, it was hard for Esparanza to live on five acres.

The power I felt from Esparanza as we worked together was intense. It was hard writing fast enough to keep up with the images she was sending.

Humans move us - from our wild living space. Why humans - no ask? I many seasons cycles lead mare. I taken - no humans ask - I want go? Members my herd taken with me. Younger members - our herd.	seasons cycles = many years

Human mare - fought big power - us back to wild living space. Big power - place young stallion - back wild living space. Big power thought - I many seasons cycles - I need humans care - I carry foal.

human mare = Judy
big power = U.S. Forest Service

I depressed - confined space. Big power - grant human mare - my care. I moved - humans open land space.

Human mare - respect my wildness. Foal birth - open space - no humans. Human mare - respect wild way. Foal - I - no forced human hands our bodies.

She and her foal were not touched by Judy.

Foal suns on land. I walk foal - humans mare sitting.

My gift - human mare.

When the foal was a few days old, Esparanza walked him to where Judy was sitting to show her. Judy felt honored.

Many seasons cycles of me - I may no survive - raise foal. In herd - I die - mare raise foal. Raise in herd. Life foal continue - no me. Foal care - I place human mare. Human mare - respect wild horses. Human mare - speak of us big power. Human mare - speak of us - other humans.

Judy spoke to the Forest Service and other humans on behalf of the wild horses.

Dying close. I ask - wild horse way - my own rhythm.

She does not want to be put down.

Rhythm life - wild - clear. My body - move slower slower. Body systems slower - prepare body stop moving - spirit move out.

Human mare agree - my leaving - own rhythm. Human worry thoughts - suffering.

What suffering? I no know. Why humans - no allow horses - die horse rhythm? What frightens humans? We no understand - human thought hurry rhythm - end body life. Body dies - spirit moves on. Simple.

Why humans fear - discomfort? Why fear - dying rhythm? We ask humans consider - why fear? We ask humans - expand humans sight of death - horse way. We teach humans - wholeness of being. We offer.

I peaceful my leaving. Why humans assume being with humans - best way? Humans - consider - we lived many many seasons cycles. Seasons cycles - we live whole - away of humans disturbance - our rhythm. Our herds live well - we whole being.

Humans squeezing of us - disruption our living way. We well - living our rhythms.

humans squeezing us = less land area

Why humans - need control our way life?

We ask - humans consider.

Esparanza did not die. She gradually accepted being confined and continued raising her foal, a colt. In the spring of 2005, Esparanza, her foal, and the other members of her herd were released on a wild horse preserve where they could live wild again. Judy had made this promise to them, and she moved heaven and earth to keep it.

La Jarita Wild Horses

September 5, 2004

I went to La Jarita Mesa in the El Rito Ranger District and sat on a tree stump near a fairly fresh pile of manure. The horses were not in sight, but I could feel them watching me. They were curious about me since they had had no contact with a human who could see in pictures like they did.

We live here - many seasons cycles. We knew - human captivity. Act of nature gave us our freedom.

Time of Spanish exploration, some of the imported Spanish horses were released into the wild by an act of nature.

We knew humans care of us - providing food - easy way. Our hearts - no forgot wild rhythm. Wild rhythm life - our true nature.

Our release - wild place - we our care. Rhythm human contact - service - melted from us. Some us easier adjust. Some us missed human hands. Adjustment took- moons - seasons. Our bodies grew fitter - hard. Our natural instincts grew sharper. Our inner system finer - of alert danger. Our eyes - grew wary. Our nostrils - receive scents keenly.

We learned scent danger - cost of us. Some us - less adaptable fell early. Some of us - wild nature intact fared better. We grew - blending rhythm of land we lived. We grew - wary. Memories of human hands - faded.

cost of us = were killed

Our first foals born - of freedom - knew no human scent - hands. First foals - saw curious images - in dams thoughts - of beings no recognize. No two legged beings of our place of living. Foals born of first foals - saw no two legged beings of dams thoughts.

First seasons toll of us. Predators brought some down. Injuries toll of us - we learned new land. Learning way of holes - drop offs - trees - rocks.

Ones of us - missing humans - failed early - second full turn of seasons - none alive. Ones missing humans - found contact of humans - wonder of merging. Ones missing humans - gift of service - gracious. Ones missing humans - new land - harsh. Ones missing humans - memories in our cells - now season.

wonder of merging = working with humans

now season = today

Suns - moons - seasons cycles - our numbers dwindled. Our bodies instincts adapting complete - our numbers grew. Mares developed deeper lead skills. Stallions stronger skills - defending - breeding.

Our numbers grew - bands break away original herd. We ranged further. Many seasons passage - found us covering great areas surface.

Our wild nature - fully forward. We lived simply - long seasons passed. No human - scent on air.

Slowly - change came.

Human scent floated to us. Stirring some of us - long forgotten images - buried deep our cells. Some us - curiosity born. Others of us - signal flight - upper most.

Dance between us - humans - began again.

Humans took us - humans way - force. Humans - forget ask. Humans thought - humans right - of us. Human will over our rhythm of us.

Memories our cells awakened - some us - old agreement of service.

Those of us taken - relearning life - humans way. Some us fare better. Some us missing rhythm - life freedom of movement.

Some us fought - dying so. Preferring death - no service.

Humans - red/brown skin - scent more of wild essence. Humans - pale skin - sharper scent - sharper thoughts. Pushing nature. Red/brown humans allowing nature.

red/brown skin = Native Americans

pale skin = white pioneers and settlers

We service of red/brown humans - easily. Red/brown humans - closer us of spirit. Pale humans - thought patterns - boxes. Red/brown humans - thought patterns - flowing edges.

boxes = rigid thought patterns.

Box thought patterns - hard understand of us. Flowing edge thought patterns - easier of us.

Why pale humans - live boxes? Why pale humans - place boxes on land - long lines? Boxes stop movement. Why pale humans - stop movement? Movement uncomfortable of pale humans?

live boxes = ridged structures, stationary

long lines = fences

Why red/brown humans - live movement - pale humans - live boxes?

Disturbance - red/brown humans - pale humans. Box thoughts - overpower - flowing thoughts. Flowing thoughts humans - confined smaller areas. Box thoughts humans - move bigger area - power over.

power over = take over power of the area

Many many - suns - moons - seasons move. Our area grows - smaller. Our numbers less less. We pushed farther away - areas harder survival.

Box thoughts humans - place slow thoughts animals areas we use. Box thoughts humans - higher thought slow thought animals - lower thoughts of us.

slow thoughts animals = cattle

Cattle were valued more than horses.

Our preference - remain wild. Allowed live rules nature. Living within cycles of seasons. We ask humans of power - consider. Humans of power no let us be - we ask humans of power work with us.

Some us - memories of service. Some us come out of wild - do service of humans. Some us - want stay wild.

Humans of power - learn listen of us. We show humans - ones of us come out - ones of us stay wild. Listening of us - humans learn - listen other humans.

We taken away our home - no asking us - hard of us. Asking us - leaving easier of us. We ask humans - takers of us - remember. Big adjustment - us lose wild way living freedom. Allow us suns - moons - adjust pace - human boxes way living. Treat us - respect - our beingness. We ask.

Our outer freedom - mirror human - inner freedom.

Their pictures were a total surprise. I assumed these horses would only show me the roundup and culling by the Forest Service. I was amazed to see these horses' cellular memories of the transition from Spanish domesticity to living wild. Their distinction between the ways of the Native Americans—red/brown humans to the horses—and the white pioneers and settlers—pale humans—was also powerful. I sat on that stump for quite awhile after the images stopped, doing my best to trust what I saw.

Wild Horse Mesa Wild Horses

September 6, 2004

There were many bands of wild horses living on Wild Horse Mesa in the San Luis Valley, Colorado. I was sitting at the edge of the mesa in the dirt and goat-head thorns. My feet were dangling over the edge of a 300-foot drop-off, and the view was glorious. Across a couple of miles of flat ground and partially dry reservoir, the mountains rose 5,000 feet high right out of the floor of the plain.

Below me, there were areas of mud and fingers of water that extended from the reservoir into the dry area. I could see tracks where horses had come to drink. Like the day before at La Jarita, I saw no horses, but could feel their presence. I began to see pictures.

No need see us. We here. Hearing us - important of us.

We live here - freedom. Humans of power - welcome our presence. Our wildness honored. Suns - moons many - no so. We were driven edge - no life of us. Our numbers - few. Humans pressed us - edge disappearance of us.

humans of power = land owners

New humans - come. New humans - joyful hearts - see us. We taken - stopped. New humans - drink our wild nature.

Tension left us. Tension left area we roam. Our numbers - slowly grow.

Past pressure of humans nature - big burden upon us. In now sun - moons - we live natures governing. Rhythm sun - water - seasons cycles - we live rhythm of.

We wear sun - warming our bodies. We wear cool - non sun air flowing over our bodies. We wear - air moving fast over our bodies. Our manes - tails - flying. Fast moving air encourages us run - our hooves dancing over earth. Our hooves barely touching earth. Barely feeling uneven earth - rocks - grass - small trees - under our hooves.

Season of small warmth our bodies - slow inner rhythm. Slow season - small warmth. Food less. Our bodies - lighter - good feeling. Hunger - rhythm of small warmth season. Hunger - sharpens senses. Hunger season - balances our numbers. Humans forget - importance of hunger season. No balance of hunger season - our numbers exceed earth food.

Humans placing food - hunger season - no rhythm of us - earth.

Humans putting hay out disturbs the wild way of balancing herd numbers.

Natures rules appear harsh - humans seeing. Us - rhythm of life. Life experience - we grow maturity - body - spirit.

Our nature - horse. We live horse life of cycles. Our horse life cycles blend - land - water - air - cycles seasons. Our horse nature entwines - land - air - water - cycles. We breathe air - air breaths us. We consume land - land consumes us. We drink water - water drinks us. Rhythm within rhythm.

Humans forget - lifes rhythms. Humans - wanting box rhythms. Rhythms - no flourish - in box.

Humans sight of wild horses - helps humans remember - rhythm inside humans. Inner human rhythm fluid - free of boxes.

Humans - see us dance with earth - remember - freedom humans are.

Land we dance on - sacred place of being. We grateful humans of power - welcome us here.

Flood of humans no stopped completely. Flood softly directed. Moving direction mutual benefit.

More humans moving into the area.

With soft direction, humans and horses benefit living in the same area.

The images stopped and I finished writing. A soft breeze moved over me. The beauty of the place and the horses that lived there completely surrounded me in their dance of life.

The difference in what each band of wild horses showed me was surprising. I don't know what I thought they would reveal, but what they gave me was more than I had expected. What they hold in their cell memories is fascinating.

I ask what it is that we humans feel we need so badly that we push aside other beings from their place of living: For control? Out of fear there is not enough to go around? For financial success? Because it is our right to dominate?

I don't know the answers. I am not a rancher whose livelihood depends on the slim margin of the cattle market. I am not a bureaucrat whose job depends on finding answers to questions that do not have easy answers, and who has to please opposing interest groups. I am not an oil field engineer who is expected to bring in oil wells in remote areas for his employer. I am not a farmer whose livelihood depends on the crops planted.

I don't know how it feels for these people, since I have no experience of what they face or of their point of view. I can, however, put the wild horses' point of view forward as they show it to me.

I believe if humans are willing to sit down and communicate with each other, ways can be found to manage our wild herds better. The solutions may be different than what we currently think. The horses are continuously showing me things that are not always what I thought them to be. They are teaching me to look outside the box of what I know and allow myself to go into the unknown, even if it feels uncomfortable.

I do know that we *need* to find solutions to wild horse management issues, or there will be no more wild horses. I asked the wild horses how it is for them to disappear. This was their answer.

We hold no fixed view. We no attached - humans way.

Experience - wild horse way life - valuable. Experience - wild horse disappear - we find experience living - another body form.

Humans loss - greater. Our loss - no as great.

Wild horses help humans - remember freedom - inside humans. Wild horses help humans - remember share.

Wild - freedom find own food - water. Wild - freedom find own shelter. Wild - freedom breed - according wild horse rules. Wild - freedom herds form - reform. Wild - freedom die - our own rhythm death. Wild - freedom born - our own rhythm birth.

Wild - live life moment - moment.

Life moment - moment - freedom of past - future.

Wild - live now moment. Next moment - next moment. Next moment die - we die. Next moment hungry - we hungry. Simple.

Wild - no guarantee - next moment.

We no wild - human care - humans land small space.

Wild horses are being put on small acreages, in human care. This is not wild to them.

Wild is wild. Human care is human care.

Wild - we choose our living way.

Human care - humans choose our living way.

As the wild horses showed me this last piece, the images were strong, clear and powerful. Their point of view is different from humans. They do not see themselves as victims. There is such a total sense of who they are in themselves as wild horses. They clearly have their own sense of self with their own concepts of life and death. There is a proud, almost noble, aura around them.

The wild horses have certainly given me something to contemplate. One thing I definitely see now is that my emotions about them do not match how they view their lives or themselves.

Wild Herd Lead Mare

February 21, 2006

I had worked with this wild herd a couple of years ago, establishing a connection with them. I found them asking me to hear what they wanted humans to know; of course, I agreed.

They all sent images at once, which was overwhelming for me. I asked for one horse to work with me, and their lead mare stepped forward.

We waited - head talker human - listen of us now.	When they asked me, I was slow in opening to them. They let me know they did not want to wait!
Why humans - move us - keep us small space land of bigger space?	Fenced out of a bigger land area.
Why humans mind - small way see us?	Why don't humans see them as capable beings.
We beings - knowing our care of our bodies. Why humans - no see - our care our bodies? We survive many many moons - seasons cycles - our care our bodies.	
Humans disrupt our living place. Humans take our food off land. Humans push us to - disappear.	Pictures of humans coming into areas where they lived and pushing them out, killing some of them with guns.
Humans stings weaken our life force. Humans poison our food with human created food.	humans stings = drug shots
Our bodies move no balance - human interference. Our bodies no creating foals. Our life force weak - no grow foals of us now.	
Human pressure of our lives push us close - disappear.	
We pushed of dying. We dying all - we disappear.	

Humans take sections of us. Humans mind - want create us - outside us creating us.

take sections of us = DNA samples
outside us creating us = cloning

Why humans mind - want create us - humans way? Why our way - ignored? Our way - our bodies whole alive movement rhythm. Humans way - our bodies die - slowly slowly.

Our spirit - low. We close edge cliff - jumping off releasing us - bondage of humans - no eyes - no ears hear us.

jumping off releasing us = dying

We call - humans hear us. Humans no hear - no see. Humans hear - see humans way.

Humans no understand - wild. Wild creates - our choosing. We no wild now. Humans choosing.

We disappear - no worry of us. No hardship of us. We disappear - we find new form express us.

Humans kill us. Humans no see - humans kill us - humans - no hear - no see.

We hold our small space - unknown seasons cycles. We hold tenuously our life now.

We wait humans - hear. Humans - no hear - we go. One - one we go. All gone - disappear.

Humans heads wonder? Where horses go? Humans no see us. Humans loss of us. Humans loss. No our loss.

We have spoken.

We ask - head talker human - show humans - our pictures.

I was almost knocked from my chair by the intensity of this mare's pictures. Her sense of urgency was very strong. I let her know I would include what she showed me in this book, thus enabling other humans to hear her message. I can find no words to describe the feeling of working with this mare and feel honored she trusted me to share her views.

Humans pushed this herd of wild horses out of their living space. The good intentions of humans to save them by using human methods such as vaccinations and taking DNA samples are pushing them to extinction. These wild horses would rather jump off a cliff and die than be managed so closely by humans. They feel their disappearance is more a loss to humans than to themselves.

More San Luis Wild Horses

March 30, 2006

I went back to the San Luis Valley and met a person who lived several miles south of the village of San Luis. He invited me to follow him to his home. On the way, we spotted a small band of wild horses in an area of scrub pine and grass about 250 feet from the edge of the narrow dirt road we were on.

I pulled over, parked, and slowly got out of the car. The horses' heads came up, looking at me. We were fascinated with each other. The lead mare was surprised I could see her pictures, and a ripple went through the band of ten horses.

This mare was proud that she was wild. She showed me clearly I was to stay where I was. I was quiet for a few minutes, then I thanked them for letting me see them. I returned to my car and continued towards this person's house.

When we pulled into his 600-foot driveway, I saw a young mare and stallion standing on the left, about half way to the house. These horses came away from the scrub pine and into the two open acres in front of the house. They quietly watched me, curious about the new human. They walked up the slight incline, stopping about ten feet from me. I was amazed they came so close. Then my host put two flakes of hay beside the house, and the horses immediately went to eat.

I had to laugh. I thought I had wild horse charisma! The real reason they came close was the hay. I was watching them eat when the mare moved away from the hay and stopped in front of me. She immediately began sending me images. The stallion was too busy alternating among eating, chasing the family dogs and showing off.

Wild mare

Bay. 3 years old.

Human - how is - living humans space?

I showed this mare she would have regular food and water, but much less space to roam. She would be touched, have things put on her body and have to do what humans wanted.

All humans listen?

I showed her that only a small number of humans could listen to horses.

Why no allowed roam - humans space way?

I showed her that humans keep horses in fences to keep them safe and close to the humans.

Humans give food?

I showed her that humans put food and water inside the barriers where the horses live.

Humans touch me?

I showed her that humans would touch her and put human devices on her body.

No big space move?

I showed her that she would have a much smaller space to move, with a barrier to keep her in this space.

With this, she went back to eating. I could feel her torn between a wild life and a life with humans. I talked to the homeowner and told him what the mare had showed me. The giving of hay and water was well intentioned, as the mare was doing poorly at the beginning of the winter.

However, the mare showed me that she was losing the edge of her wildness and was becoming dependent on the hay and water provided by the human. This young mare was missing the company of mares in a band. The stallion's company was too intense at times. My host mentioned he had noticed that the mare had disappeared several times lately.

This mare and stallion were losing their fear of these humans who would soon be moving. We discussed weaning the young horses off of provided hay and water. We wanted to prepare them for the next humans who would live in this house who may not want wild horses so close.

Lead mare

On the drive out, I saw the same band of horses I had encountered on my drive in. They were standing in a meadow. The mare who had noticed me earlier looked my way and started sending pictures.

No human ways - bind me.

I flow movement. Moving slowly - eating earth growth. Moving to water many many movements.

many many movements = walking steps, miles to water

I follow season rhythm - food - water - shelter.

Human food - binds horse movement - human space.

Humans - small movement.

Wild movement - rhythm our life - movement horse way.

Humans forget - life movement - no barriers.

Wild movement - no human barriers.

This mare liked her life. She was independent and free to find her own food and water. She was free of human barriers. It was clear the food humans gave had a price—loss of movement, loss of choice where food, water and shelter were to be found and general loss of choice in living her own life. Life with humans would be a loss of independence and freedom.

It might be interesting to think about how we humans lose experiences by playing it safe and not choosing to live our lives full out. My time with these wild horses opened my eyes to seeing beyond ease and comfort.

The young mare and stallion were slowly losing their independence. The horses showed me that living wild is a delicate balance between life and death. Wild is independence and freedom, even if it means death from lack of food or water. We need to weigh our actions carefully, even though the actions are meant in kindness.

Considerations

Wild horses have certainly shaken up my view of what is wild. It is hard to choose between allowing another being to live a life of their own choosing, and stepping in with kind intent to help these beings by giving them food and other comforts. I am not saying either one is right or wrong.

For me, I have been challenged in how I think and act on wild horse issues. I am able to look at the horse's point of view and see something different from my own. It is important to understand humans often take their view of life and project it onto horses. From the horses' point of view, wild is a lifestyle.

I leave you with these questions: What is wild? What is domesticated? They are good questions to ask.

Chapter 9

Pain & Illness

I was visiting friends in Pennsylvania in October of 2004 and had the pleasure of working with their horses, who were eager to show me about pain and illness. It struck me as odd at the time because I did not know my dad was sick. Within a few days, I went to visit my family in New York with no idea what awaited me. My sister picked me up and told me our Dad was in the ICU unit at the local hospital.

While at the hospital, I was exposed to more TV, newspapers and magazines than usual. I noticed how much advertising is devoted to pain relief. In my many hours at the hospital, I saw how much pain-related medicines were dispensed. The information the horses gave me helped greatly to deal with what unfolded with my Dad.

My own experiences with numerous horse-related accidents had taught me a great deal about how I dealt with pain in my own body. Due to my body's high sensitivity to pain-relieving drugs, I am unable to use them. This allows my body to use its innate ability to manage pain, just like the horses do.

More than a year later, writing the introduction for this chapter, I finally understood why the horses showed me about pain and illness when they did. I couldn't see it then as I was too consumed with my Dad's dying.

Listening to horses over the last eight years, I have learned a lot about what it is like for them when they have pain and illness, what they call discomfort and body disruption. It is a common subject in my translation work. In this chapter you will see the horses' point of view on discomfort and body disruption. It is very interesting.

Khmira Bey, Momenta, Cimarron, Sara Grey

Khmira Bey - Arabian mare. Bay. Late teens.

Momenta - Mare. Chestnut. Teens.

Cimarron - Thoroughbred gelding. Chestnut. Late 20's.

Sara Grey - Arabian mare. Gray. Teens.

October 8, 2004

I was sitting in my friend's kitchen having breakfast when the horses came and stood by the fence. They were looking up at the house, which is on a hill above the barn and pastures. I grabbed my notebook and went down to the pasture to sit with them. The horses in this group were older, and some had serious health issues. Following is what they wanted me to know.

We ask - show pictures. We remember - feeling of mare human.	I worked with these horses six months ago.
We want told - feel of us. We disruptions - our bodies.	disruptions = illnesses
Disruptions of our bodies - cause humans discord of feeling. We no understand - humans discord of feeling - disruption of our bodies.	discord of feeling = emotions
Disruption - discomfort - part life of bodies. Why humans mind - think - life body - no disruption - no discomfort? Life - no so. Life is bumps - disruption - discomfort. Body always perfect - no learning. Body disruption - discomfort - learning experience.	discomfort = pain learning experience = expansion of awareness
Why humans large discord feelings - we discomfort our bodies? Why humans - fearful body discomfort?	

Humans forget - way of inner discomfort management? We allow discomfort - part life in body. Discomfort - simply is of us. Some us more sensitive of discomfort. We no dwell - our discomfort. We allow - discomforts movement - within us. We adjust - our outward movement - to level of discomfort.

Is simple - waiting - being of discomfort - body repairs disruption. Humans rush - repairing our bodies. We stay in rhythm - repairing movement our bodies. We no discord feeling - suns - repairing our bodies. Repairing level = function survival.

repairing level =
level of repairing is based on survival

Wild living - level function repairing - higher. Living humans care - our bodies less high level - repairing for survival. Repairing no go higher level - no necessary - body survival humans care. Food brought to us - humans living. Human place living - outer movement of body - no critical survival of body - as in wild living place.

Humans like close care of us. Some us give humans opportunity - exercise humans need. Humans mind - need - enjoy figuring riddles out. We provide riddles of disruption - discomfort - for humans solve. Clever of us. We serve humans - well.

Their humor made me laugh! The images of humans examining horses trying to figure out the problem were a riot.

Humans need - complicated - disruption - discomfort of us - so humans feel important - we easily comply.

Again their humor is so funny.

Of us - disruption - no disruption - no concern of us. Discomfort - no discomfort - no concern. Life is life. Breathing - no breathing - no concern. Moment is moment. Sun is sun. Moment - moment - make sun. Sun - sun - make moon. Moon - moon - make season. Season - season make season cycle. Whole cycle - whole cycle body life - rhythm body release to

breathing - no breathing = death is no concern.

Horses have no concept of time. The closest I can come with them is suns, moons and seasons cycle.

body release to earth = birth

earth. Body slow to - no breathing. No breathing body - blends to earth. Essence of us breaths. *We - moment rhythm. Moment rhythm of us important. Moment rhythm - disruption - discomfort - simple moment rhythm of us. Easy of us.* *Human discord of feeling - we feel - deeply - our beingness. Humans discord of feeling - hard of us. We no inner mechanism - deflect away humans discord of feeling. Humans discord of feeling - disrupts our flow of moment.* *Why humans - many discords of feelings? Why humans - no trust our body rhythms repairing? Why humans - push repairing? Repairing move own rhythm of us.* *We ask - humans consider.*	body slow = age essence breaths = spirit

Blossom

Quarter Horse mare. Dark bay. 10 years old.

February 22, 2006

Blossom had been on a long regimen of drugs. She showed me how she felt about what humans were doing to help her.

Humans liquid stings - hinder our bodies ability - regulating discomfort. *Long use liquid stings - impedes our ability - of internal balance inner movement. Impedes our management discomfort.* *Short use - breaks circles. Long use creates - downward functioning spiral - our inner movement.*	humans liquid stings = drug shots

Life is trade offs.

Why humans - no use discomfort? Why humans - no use discomfort - look deep inside humans - see unbalanced rhythm - find balanced rhythm.

Liquid stings - disturb inner balance rhythm. Disabling inner movements ability regulate inner balance.

Blossom wanted me to know the drugs used to manage her discomfort over a long period of time had affected her own ability to manage the discomfort. She showed me her inner movements were out of balance due to prolonged use of the drugs. Short-term use could break a cycle of discomfort. Long-term use lessened her own ability to manage her discomfort. The short-term application had a benefit, while the long-term use had a more adverse, long-term effect.

Blossom was curious why humans do not use discomfort to look inside to find an unbalanced rhythm and then find the balanced rhythm. She saw discomfort as a part of life and something to be used rather than avoided. She represented the horses' point of view, which I have been shown many times by many different horses.

CONSIDERATIONS

The horse's view of pain and illness was an eye opener. Humans feel the need to fix pain or illness immediately. Sometimes this goes against the horse's own repairing movement. The horses are asking us not to project our human emotions of pain and illness on them. Horses are different.

It does not mean that humans should do nothing. The horses are showing us their way of coping is simply different. They don't try to avoid pain and illness—they simply live with what comes along. Horses live in the moment and do not worry what will happen tomorrow. Their life is happening now, now, now….

Chapter 10

Slaughter

The topic of horse slaughter is difficult, emotionally charged and a current political issue.

I have spent some interesting time with horses who were in killer pens at auctions and then bought by people intent on saving them from slaughter. After being taken from the auction grounds, they were occasionally put in temporary homes until a permanent placement could be found. What these horses had to show me was surprising.

Before you read this chapter, put aside your emotions and opinions and read with an open mind and heart. The horses express themselves clearly, so I will leave it to them.

Sadie

Quarter Horse mare. Gray. 6 years old.

January 30, 2005

Friends asked me to work with a mare they were buying from a man who bought her out of the killer's pen at an auction. The man was surprised to find her in the killer's pen because she had good conformation, was sound, had no blemishes and had registration papers.

Knowing he could not keep Sadie himself, he called my friends who were immediately interested in adding her blood lines to their breeding program. The plan was to breed her since she was in heat, and then ship her to Texas where she would join their band of pregnant mares.

My friends were worried because Sadie was listless. There were 30 mares in the barn, and she showed no interest in any of them. She just stood with her head down in the corner of her stall.

At the barn, the mares looked at me with interest as I walked by their stalls. Sadie however, did not move. She looked like a statue with her back to the stall door. I stood quietly, letting her know I could hear her, if she gave me permission. I slid the door open a few feet and stepped just inside. Sadie turned her head slightly to me, having a hard time grasping I could see horse pictures. We stood in that position many minutes. Sadie had never met a human who could hear horses, and she wasn't sure she could trust me.

I asked her if I could come closer. She showed me to stay where I was. I stood with my hands at my sides. We stayed like that for more minutes. Sadie finally picked her head up, sighed and turned slightly towards me. I still stayed put. She sighed again and took a step closer. I showed her I would listen if she had something to share, but would not force her in any way. More time passed.

Slowly, Sadie worked herself all the way over to me. She blew into my face, and I blew into her nostrils. Ever so gently, she touched the side of my face with her muzzle. She showed me I could touch her neck. The tension left her as I stroked her neck, and her pictures started to come. I picked up my notebook from just outside the stall door, sat on my bucket and started writing.

I was a bit surprised as Sadie showed me about slaughter. Here is what she had to say.

Human way - taking our bodies. We give freely - use our bodies.

human way taking our bodies = slaughter

Wild way living - our bodies - support life other beings. Is way life - prey body being.

prey body being = horses are prey animals

Why humans - see death of us - humans created - box leaving place as worse wild wolf run us down - eat of our body - no dead completely.

box leaving place = slaughter house

To them not any worse than a wolf killing them.

We givers - is our nature.

Some animals - takers. Is their nature. Takers - use of givers.

Simple balance life.

Humans takers.

We see - no difference - shape of takers.

Wolf shape - coyote shape - mountain lion shape - human shape - all takers.

Takers - balance - numbers givers.

Humans - create numbers of us - more us earth sustain. More us - humans use for. More us - humans places live.

More horses than there are places for in the human's world.

Humans takers - balance our numbers - doing takers way.

Our movement survival - survival deep movement our bodies.

No fear death - is survival movement body. Survival movement body - no fear us dying. Humans fear - dying.

The survival mechanism of the body is very powerful and works till the last breath is taken. Horses are clear there is a difference between the survival mechanism and fear.

We in our body - alive - out our body - dead. Simple way of us.

We ask humans - respect us - humans created box leaving place. Respectful taking us - calmer of us. We respected - easier way - going of us.

Why our violent death worse - humans violent death - cows violent death?

Images of humans at war with each other. They get those images from us.

Life is violent components. Act of mare body pushing foal body into life violent movement - movement life.

Life balance - movement - smooth - sharp. Why humans - want smooth? Life no smooth - is so.

Humans create us - big numbers.

All us - no room stay. Is so - wild living. Is so - human living.

Beings move off earth - balance living.

We ask humans - aware role - taker. Is no bad - is way is.

Simple of us.

The images stopped. I realized Sadie had become the collective speaker on the slaughter topic for horses in general. The atmosphere in the stall was calm and matter-of-fact. Their point of view was very clear. There was no anger, blame or negative emotion. She showed me that life was about balances. To the horses, humans play a part in maintaining those balances. I showed Sadie I would tell other humans. She sighed and started eating hay.

CONSIDERATIONS

The horses see humans as predators fulfilling their role as predators. They remind us that predators help control the numbers of prey animals. Balancing numbers of prey animals helps maintain the balance of food and water available.

Put your emotions aside, as I had to do, and ask yourself these questions. If all the horse slaughter facilities in the U.S. were closed, where would the horses destined for those facilities go? Where would they be housed? Where would the food and water come from to take care of them? Where does the money come from to house, care and feed them? Who is going to care for all these horses?

The horses are asking us to think about the answers to these questions. They are asking us to think about the numbers of horses created by us every year. Horses are not creating the problem with the numbers of horses—humans are.

This chapter brought me up short. The horses forced me to look at it from their point of view. When I went to work with Sadie, I never dreamed this is what she would show me. I was a very sobered human when I left her stall.

When we want to breed a mare and create a foal, we might want to start asking ourselves these questions:

> What will happen to this foal?
> Who will be responsible for its life as it grows into a horse?
> Who will care for it when it reaches its average life expectancy of 20 to 25 years?

Our horses are asking us to look past our emotions and take a serious look at what we are doing. On the surface, it appears noble to promote stopping the slaughter of horses. However, the horses are showing us we have a responsibility as predators to limit the overpopulation of horses. How we see our responsibility is up to us. They have my attention.

Chapter 11

School Horses & Jobs

As a long-time riding instructor, I was grateful to the horses and ponies in the school string. Each horse and pony who came to us had its own background and story. Some were backyard horses, while others were former top-level three-day eventers, dressage horses, open jumpers, show hunters, rodeo horses or race horses. There were many reasons for their owners letting them go.

These horses were of different colors and sizes and had their own personalities. They were truly my partners in teaching adults and children to ride. All of them were patient and took good care of their riders.

We had a wonderful former three-day eventer named Schubert. He geared himself to each rider. For a young child, he would do everything slowly. For an advanced adult, he would come to life, jumping brilliantly. He had a funny way of letting us know he wanted an extra day off. Schubert would come to the center of the ring and stand near me, even though his rider tried very hard to keep him on the rail. His look said it all. If his request were ignored, he would act up, but not enough to unseat his rider. He would get his extra day off. The day he was retired from the school string we threw a party for him—there was not a dry eye in the barn.

Of all the jobs a horse can do, I have much respect and love for the school horses. They are heroes who do their jobs well. I will now turn the chapter over to our horse teachers.

Joe's School Horses

January 15, 2005

I went to Virginia to visit my friend Joe, a professional horseman. He was managing a farm with a riding school that specialized in teaching beginners to ride. It was a very active program with students ranging from four to sixty years of age.

While there, I worked with some of Joe's clients and their horses. It brought back many memories of my teaching days. It was fun to be in the barn while a group of six young children, mostly seven-year-olds, got their horses and ponies ready as part of their lesson. I lent a helping hand when one child could not reach high enough to put on the saddle, and helped another with a bridle when the pony had its jaw clamped tight. The young woman teaching the class was managing quite well but was glad of an extra pair of helping hands. She had a no-nonsense approach and gave clear directions to the children in her charge.

While I was assisting, a couple of the horses and ponies realized I could see their pictures. They were curious about me and took the opportunity to show me things they wanted people to know about being school horses. A pony named Patches took over sending me pictures.

Patches

Grade pony gelding. Piebald. 12 years old.

Patches was handsome, smart and a perfect size for children. He carried his charge carefully with enough spunk to be fun but not enough to be scary—the right mix for educating his young riders. Patches enjoyed being adored by his students.

We want humans know - ponies - horses - working teaching humans sit upon us - we special service of humans.

We many colors - shapes - sizes - ages. We no perfect shape - humans high regard. No - our service teaching humans - sit upon us - no humans know - sit upon perfectly formed horses - ponies - carry humans - humans created jobs.

Pictures of perfectly shaped show horses. Without school horses' service, humans would not know how to sit on the perfectly formed horses.

Is hard work - carry humans bodies - humans learn balance sit - hands steering us.

Humans bodies clumsy - compared - fluid movement of us. Humans mind think - we stupid - let humans sit upon us - direct us - jobs humans create. Humans mind - no know our nature. Humans heart - feels our nature.

Humans mind assume - we stupid - allowing humans use of us. Humans mind think - superior of us.

We beings - of service. We generous - our service of humans. We serve - our choice.

Our association with humans - part our evolvement our spirit. Our contact of humans - we experience humans nature - all beings evolve to.

We choose - teach humans - humans no force us work. We possess - strength of body - far exceeding - humans strength of body. Largest - strongest humans - no power hold us - we choose no be held.

Humans hold snakes attached straps our heads - we choose run - humans no stop us.

snakes = reins
straps our heads = bridle

Balancing humans sitting upon us - new to sitting upon us - we skillful balancing. We know difference feel - level humans experience - sitting upon us.

Less experienced human sitting upon us - wobbles - shaky movements - abrupt movements.

We adjust - our steps - help wobbly human sit upon us. Human wobbles to side - we shift under human - stay under human - catch human.

Helping humans learn - we do humans ask - asked correctly. No ask correctly - we no move. We teach - humans be focused - precise humans directions of us. Important of us - humans learn focus - precise directions.

Humans afraid of us - we show fear back - to humans. Many humans - afraid of us. Humans afraid - human emits - sharp jagged energy - humans confused thought patterns. Humans confused thought patterns - hard us understand.

Big effort of us - function steady - humans confused thoughts - wobbly abrupt body movements.

Some us sore backs - devices humans place our backs - pinch us. Improper sitting devices - discomfort. We pin ears - alert humans - we discomfort - sore - humans think we bad.

Why - no humans - look at devices?

Our bodies - adjust shape - less blood flow muscle. Muscle grow smaller - less blood.

Over time, improperly fitting saddles cause the muscle to atrophy.

The pictures stopped. The class was over, and the students dismounted in the indoor arena. They walked their mounts back to the barn to unsaddle and groom before putting them back in their stalls. Patches looked very pleased with himself when I went to where he was being untacked by the child who had ridden him.

Flower

Grade Quarter Horse-type mare. Chestnut, star. Late teens.

January 20, 2005

I visited the riding school again today. As I walked down the barn aisle, an older mare named Flower caught my attention. The owners of this farm bought her from an auction and put her into the riding school string after spending some time working with her. She wanted me to come into her stall and immediately started sending pictures. I got my notebook and a bucket on which to sit.

Many us - throw away horses. Humans way - looking.	
Why humans - hold images - perfect shape of us - humans want us be?	
We no perfect shape - humans think us less. We less important - humans mind. Us less important - go humans place - humans learn sit upon us.	humans place = riding school
Our view - horses teaching humans - hold high value - our looking view. Our high value - higher level service - us teach humans sitting upon us.	Horses give teaching a high value.
Our service of humans - is service of horses. More humans learn of us - more of us - clearer contact with humans.	clearer contact with humans = clearer understanding

Flower was very proud of her job in the riding school string. She saw that helping humans learn to ride properly would help other horses when these same humans rode them. She clearly held the idea that even though she was not the most beautiful horse, she was still important. For every top-level horse in whatever discipline you may choose, there are many more horses that serve and do their jobs brilliantly. I want to acknowledge these horses for their gracious service to humans.

Flower had a lovely, quiet way about her, with soft, kind eyes. I feel honored to have known her. I am happy to serve her by taking the time to write her message on school horses. My friend Joe is the only other human she has ever met who can hear her.

Flower's Additional Message

It was the day before I was to go back to Colorado, and I was walking down the barn aisle. As I passed Flower's stall, she came to the front and stared at me. She had a pinched look on her face. I looked around and noticed all the horses looked the same way. I stood in front of her and she showed me she couldn't get away from the noise. I didn't understand. She showed me again. That time I got it; the radio was playing. Flower and the rest of the horses couldn't get away from the sound of the radio.

I found Joe and asked him about the radio. He told me it played 24/7. I told him what Flower gave me and asked if the radio could be turned off. Joe said yes. I walked over and turned off the radio. The collective relief in the barn was instant. The horses all looked more relaxed. Later in the day, a few of the boarders commented that the quiet barn was nicer.

It never occurred to me that the sound of a radio playing constantly could be stressful for horses. Flower showed me their natural world is quiet, with the sounds of nature. Their view of human voices with music is just noise.

They simply want us to know their world is quieter. Humans live in a fast-paced, noisy world of their own creation. The other piece that flows from this is that in our busy, noisy world there is little room for listening. If I am in "busy-brain" or a highly emotional state, I don't hear anyone but myself. I certainly can't focus on a horse. When I am this way, I will not work with a horse. I wait until I am calm again.

I thanked Flower and showed her I would pass the message along to other humans.

Cat Queen

Quarter Horse mare. Champion cutting horse. Chestnut, no markings. Mid teens.

March 3, 2006

I visited a friend who managed a breeding farm. As we walked down the barn aisle, she pointed out a mare that had done well as a cutter. As I moved past this mare's stall, she came to her stall door and looked at me. Once this mare discovered that I could hear her, she let the pictures flow.

I smart.	
Why humans want foals? Why important of humans? Boring.	She is at this farm to be bred.
Is ok here.	
Cow moving - I like job. Watch cow move. Cow move - I know more - human know less.	
Like move cows. Good job.	
Why humans - no use us - long space. Why humans - no use us space we no want job.	long space = for a long time She wanted to be used until she did not want the cutting job anymore.
Hard of me - humans no use me - I want move cows.	
I ask - no please humans? Humans no use me?	She could not understand why she was no longer used to cut cows.
I show humans - I want cow job. Humans - no hear.	
I accept foal job. No like - cow job like.	
Human of power knows - I special.	human of power = owner
Miss cows.	
Humans learn - I like job - I do job long space.	
I ask no new job. Ok new job - old job complete.	She did not ask for a new job. A new job would be ok if she were finished with the old job.

Presents. *I teach humans - give me presents.* *I smart.*	presents = cookies, made especially for horses

This mare was a riot. She was so clear about how much she liked her job cutting cows. She knew how smart she was and was very pleased with herself for teaching humans to give her cookies, which she loved. There was a big jar filled with them outside her stall door.

Cat Queen showed me she accepted her new job of producing foals, even though she missed the action of cows. She was smart enough to let go of what she was unable to do and was okay with her current life as a brood mare.

Her gracious acceptance touched my heart. I looked at my own life and how I get stuck in the past and don't accept the present.

I sat on a bucket outside Cat Queen's fence, writing. She stood close, facing me, ears up, with a bright intelligent look in her eyes. Her sense of humor about teaching humans to give her cookies made me laugh. She let me know she expected one, which I gave her, being a trainable human. Being with her was an absolute delight. My hat is off to Cat Queen. She got lemons and made lemonade, and cookies!

CONSIDERATIONS

This chapter is touching in its simplicity. School horses see themselves as doing an important job. Humans could take lessons in graciousness from these horses.

Flower gave us a very important piece on radios and noise and I think we should take this seriously. Think about being locked in a stall and not being able to get away from constant noise. It's not very pleasant.

With a great sense of humor, Cat Queen teaches us about acceptance. We could do well to emulate our horse's simpler view of life.

Chapter 12

Weaning

Weaning is the time when a foal is permanently separated from its dam. The age for weaning varies, depending on the specific situation. In a human-managed environment, it is typically between four and seven months of age. For horses living in the wild, the process is more gradual and may take up to a year or two. The weaning process has effects on both the dam and the foal as the milk supply dries up. The foal must become self-sufficient for food and find safety and security away from its dam.

The work I did with the horses in this chapter expanded my level of awareness about weaning. This is an area of horse management in which I have very limited experience. Before this, I was oblivious to what mares and their foals went through when they were separated using our controlled horse management practices.

Once more the horses took me into their world, wanting to share their view.

Cahir

Irish Cob mare. Piebald. 6 years old.

November 13, 2005

Cahir was separated from her foal and taken to a nearby farm with a stallion in residence. She injured her left hind leg kicking at the fence, even though an empty pen separated her from the stallion. The veterinarian treating her recommended stall rest for a month. The decision was made to send Cahir to the small ranch where I lived.

She was in a pen forty feet from my front door. Her distress was obvious, so I went out to the pen. It took a little time for her to realize I had the ability to hear her. Cahir stopped pacing and stood in front of me. The rest was easy.

Why I punished?	
Why my foal moved - sharply?	Why was her foal taken from her suddenly?
Why I moved away my herd - to place I no want be. Place no want be - stallion - I no like. I kick - stallion - hard - frustration. I hurt. Humans move me - new humans place. I confined - alone. Why I alone? Is distressing.	
Why humans - take foal - no of rhythm foal move away.	
Foal moving away - is slow movement. No sharp movement. Our rhythm - prepares foal slowly. Foal need - herd protection - moons - seasons cycles. Why humans - push push us? Why humans - no understand - our rhythm of foal move away?	In the wild, a foal's weaning is a slow movement, happening over a much longer period of time.
Why humans - no listen us?	
Foal - in humans rhythm hard of us.	

We ask humans - listen us - we show humans our rhythms. Sharp humans lines - abrupt on us. Our lines - soft movement. Humans lines - sharp - stiff - no movement. Our rhythm - gentler - slower movement.	Having a foal in human's management is hard on us. sharp humans line = rigid thoughts
I want go - my herd.	
I headache - tight stomach.	
I show - human who hears - how is of me. *Human who hears - show me - I go my herd - one moon.* *I wait. Is hard alone.*	I sent her the picture of a full moon, which is four weeks, to help her know when she was going back to her herd.

I spent as much time as I could with Cahir. I took her out of her pen daily and hand-walked her, giving her the chance to see other horses. I turned her out in pens where she could graze a little. I also turned horses into a pen nearby to allow some company for part of the day.

I did my best to show Cahir she was not being punished, that I would explain to other humans how hard it is on horses to do weaning this way. She became less depressed and began to accept her situation. It also helped that I was able to let Cahir know she would be going back to her herd in a moon. As time went on, I adjusted the picture of the moon shape, letting her know she was closer to going home. She was a sweet mare, and I missed her when she went home.

Peach

Warmblood/Thoroughbred mare. Bay, wide blaze, left front & right hind socks. 12 years old.

November 18, 2005

Peach had her first foal, a colt, on May 24, 2005. His name was Finn. They lived in a pen with a shed that was part of a larger building in which I lived. The owner made the decision to wean Finn.

My udder - discomfort. Too full.

Is hard - raising foal - outside of herd. Herd - mares and foals. Is company. All mares - watch foals.

Alone - with foal. No mare company - hard of me.

I watch foal - always. Always - big alone - with foal. Rhythm of herd - support of all. We support of all - soothing. Comfort. Safety.

Sharp line - human foal taking - harsh on me. Milk flow - build up - in me. No slow lessening. Hard on my body. Hard on foal body. Is crisis mode - of our bodies. Our body rhythm - designed slow rhythm. Sharp rhythm - move us - too fast. Force body - create - no foal rhythm - hard on body.

Nursing motion for foal - Is life rhythm nurture. Life rhythm nurture - sharp line - is crisis of foals rhythm.

Nursing stops abruptly in humans' way of taking foals from their dams.

Foal miss - nursing motion. Nursing motion - own rhythm of unwind - stop. Foal confused. Miss rhythm of dam. Safety of dam. Lessons of dam. Creates hole - in foals being. Dam - foal - rhythm of nursing - two cycles of seasons.

Two years in horse rhythm.

Back with herd - comforting of me. Why - foal no come? My body no ready - no nurse foal. Support of herd - nurse foal comfort of me.

Why humans no listen?

I comfort - with herd now. Want foal with herd. Is hard.

Peach had a hard time having her foal taken from her against her natural rhythm. She enjoyed the comfort of being back with the herd, and could not understand why Finn could not come with her. I tried to soothe her as best I could.

Finn

Warmblood colt. 6 months old.

Shock - body. No dam - sharp line. *Inner rhythm - movement discord.* *Stomach rhythm discord - abrupt end milk.* *Scared - no dam. No herd. Survival. Worry.*	stomach rhythm discord = digestive tract upset

In Finn's perspective it was a shock to his body to have his dam removed abruptly. His inner body rhythms were pushed out of sync, and his stomach and digestive tract were upset with the sudden end to receiving his dam's milk.

Finn felt scared without his dam, and there was no herd to protect him. Even though he was with Miles, it was not the same. He worried about survival. Survival is at the core of a horse's existence.

Miles

Warmblood/Thoroughbred gelding. Bay, no markings.
8 years old.

Miles had surgery on his left stifle and was put in with Peach and Finn to recuperate. Being in the herd would have been too much activity for him. When Peach was taken and put back with the herd, Miles remained with Finn.

Miles was not happy babysitting Finn. He came to the fence and stared at me until I came over—he had things to get off his chest.

I angry. Angry - no go herd. Humans take mare. Foal - with me.	
Is no job - of me. Is embarrassing - of me.	Male horses do not take care of foals in the herd. It's a mare's job.
Gentle human - show me - is job humans ask - I do. I no like job. I show gentle human - young mare job. Take her. Me go - herd.	gentle human = author
Gentle human - show me - young mare - rough with foal - hurt foal.	There is a young mare in the herd.
Gentle human - show me - is important job - humans ask me. Protect foal.	
I do - as gentle human show. I protect foal. No like job.	
I miss herd.	
Mare - no like. Me - no like. Foal - confused.	All of them are upset.
Foal protection - alone - big job - no herd. Lonely job. No company of me.	
Why humans - no sense of rhythms? Make sharp lines - movement of us.	

Miles was not happy being left alone with Finn. He wanted a young mare from the herd to do the babysitting job. When we explored this option, however, the young mare was too rough with the foal. It helped Miles a bit to be shown that protecting Finn was an important job.

The happy news is that after Finn was fully weaned, Miles went to another farm. He went back in training with the same young woman he worked with before his surgery. Miles was thrilled to be away from the foal and working with the young woman he liked.

Finn went into the herd here at the ranch, and Cahir went home to her herd. She fully recovered from her injury. Even though I dealt with unhappy horses for a while, things did work out.

Herd of Pasture Mares

September 10, 2006

I was on a large ranch, and I watched from a distance while foals were taken from their dams, put in a stock trailer and driven away. The mares raced the pasture fence, chasing the trailer with their foals inside. The foals were screaming their high-pitched whinnies, and the mares were frantically whinnying back.

When the truck and trailer finally disappeared, the group of ten mares ran to the pen in the corner of the pasture where they had been separated from their foals. They stood looking and whinnying. Then the mares again ran the length of the fence calling for their foals. The pasture was about three hundred acres. When the mares could not find their foals at the pen or along the road, they ran to the south side looking and calling. These mares ran like this all over the pasture for more then an hour, finally stopping, tired and confused.

I walked to the fence on the west side as the mares were standing there whinnying to the stallion who protected them all summer. He was on the hillside nearby in a pasture he shared with four other stallions. This stallion kept calling back to them, frustrated that an irrigation ditch and two fence lines separated him from them.

I tried telepathically to open to the mares and was unsuccessful. Their distress was so high they could not hear my thoughts. Neither could the stallion. I stayed for half an hour and finally gave up in my own frustration at not being able to reach them. The running and calling went on until dark when things finally settled down.

CONSIDERATIONS

As we can see, the horses showed us how disruptive it is for them to be weaned abruptly. It has a ripple effect throughout the herd. We are being asked to find a less sharp way of weaning foals that more closely fits the horses' slower rhythms.

Chapter 13

Vaccinations

It is accepted horse management practice to vaccinate horses on a regular basis against common diseases. I had not considered vaccination as a topic for this book. It came as a surprise, therefore, when one of my friend's horses, Malt, approached and showed me he had pictures relating to vaccination.

As on other topics, the horse's views may raise some difficult discussion and questions. However, Malt wanted humans to know how horses felt when they were given vaccines. He was speaking as a representative of horses as a collective, not just for himself. Let's see what he has to say.

Malt

Foundation Quarter Horse gelding. Dark bay, no markings.
6 years old. 15.2 hands.

In the spring of 2002, Malt was vaccinated with a three-in-one injection. West Nile vaccine was not given, as this virus was little known in Colorado at that time.

In September of that year, Malt was diagnosed with West Nile virus. For the first three days, his treatment consisted of a potent anti-inflammatory, an analgesic, electrolyte paste, therapeutic-grade essential oils and nutritional support. Thereafter, the essential oils and nutritional support continued. In two weeks, he appeared almost back to normal and received follow-up work with essential oils for the next four years.

April 25, 2006

I had gone to visit my friend on her ranch. We were sitting on her porch, looking out over the pastures, and talking about this book. From out in the field, Malt caught my attention and showed me he had information for the book, but that he would let me know when he was ready to give it.

May 27, 2006

Malt finally let me know he was ready to give me his information about vaccinations. When Malt began sending pictures, there was urgency to his message that I had not felt working on other topics. This is what Malt showed me and what he and the horses, collectively, wanted humans to know.

Human liquid sting of control - overwhelms our bodies.	liquid sting of control = vaccine shot
Why humans - big fear - humans give us liquid sting of control?	What do humans fear so much about diseases to give horses vaccines?
Why humans - forget - movement rhythm of all beings dancing in accordance to each beings life rhythm?	
Why humans fear death of us to natures movement of all beings?	
Why humans create liquid sting of control?	
Liquid sting of control - damages - our bodies deeply. Liquid sting of control - damages - our bodies in our smallest being body place. Liquid sting of control - weakens our bodies - affects our life spark. Weakens - our system of defense.	smallest being body place = cells system of defense = immune system
We die of natures movement - we die. Is part bigger movement of all.	

Why humans - want control - natures movement? Why humans - fear - natures movement?

Liquid sting of control - affects our feet - our digestion. Our feet move to rid - our bodies of liquid sting of control residue - out our body.

For the horse collective, Malt showed me the inflamed laminae—the vascular layer between the bone in the hoof and the hoof wall. The laminae become inflamed as a way of forcing the chemical residue out of their bodies—a violent reaction of detoxification. Malt showed that horses' digestive tracts become unable to fully digest food properly, causing painful gas in the intestines. He also showed that there is a slow build-up of toxins in their bodies that pass from mare to foal and also affect the viability of a stallion's sperm.

Liquid sting of control - sharp movement - inside our bodies. We ask humans - create softer movement - way management of us.

We ask humans - see movement of all beings - moving in patterns of life - sharing earth.

Humans - more more protect us - from lifes movement - creates damage our body inner rhythm balance.

Why humans - see attack - only movement - solve worry?

Attack is sharp movement. Attack is fear. Why humans - no see - softer rhythm?

attack = to kill or push out of the way

Softer rhythm - creates movement - allowing our bodys inner movements balance us - wholly powerfully.

We ask humans - awareness of humans actions - in care of us. Humans - allow - hearts guide. Humans mind - sees sharp attack way.

Humans heart - sees movement of all. *Hear us.*	

July 1, 2006

I knew there was more to come from Malt for this chapter. Today he drew me to him again. It was time. Malt lifted his head and showed me to sit by the fence. Notebook in hand, we went to work.

Liquid sting of control - damage smallest being body place - beyond repair of us.	
I no fear human label.	human label = West Nile
Humans focus label - humans create.	Humans focus on the diseases they label.
Humans separate - movements of beings. Moving each beings - connection of all.	
Life movement - dance - of all touching beings together. Beings touch is so - dance life. Beings no touch is so - dance life.	
Unseen beings - dance with seen beings. Simply - movement of all.	unseen beings = virus, bacteria
Unseen beings - hold life spark.	seen beings = horses, humans, etc.
Seen beings - hold life spark.	
Seen being - die dancing with unseen beings - is movement - of seen beings life.	Simply meant to happen in this being's life.
Humans - separate movement. Separated movement - distorted. No longer connected - movement of all life. Separated movement - loses full life spark. Loss full life spark - creates discord - fear.	
Beings die - is so - way of life. Humans - fear - creates control action.	
Ocean of life - creates constant movement. Constant movement creates - birth - death. Simple. Ocean of life - creates coming - going.	

With soft eye human help. I survived human label.

soft eye human = owner

A soft eye has a broad view of life.

I experience unseen being dancing - inside my body. Created - inner experience - expanding my inner being. Experience - I chose.

I ask humans - use softer eyes. Softer eye sees - dance of all beings.

Humans attack - creates push against - unseen being. Attack - forces unseen being grow stronger - effort of survival of unseen being.

Softer eyes - creates way enhance life force - seen beings. Stronger life force - enables seen beings - dance with unseen beings. Stronger life force - helps seen beings - survive dance.

Some of us die. Is so. Soft eyes - allows give - take dance.

Some die. Some live. Simple.

I ask humans - see dance of life fully - wholly.

I ask humans - see attack damages all beings seen - unseen. No necessary.

Death - is no real death. No death occurs - of spirit. Body dies. Spirit lives always.

Humans forget. I ask - humans remember.

Humans - attack - fear - creates bigger disturbance - movement of all.

Force attack = disturbance movement.

Softer eyes = flow movement.

I ask humans - hear me.

My experience - human label - created stronger whole being of me.

Humans - hear softly.

CONSIDERATIONS

Immunization and the use of preventative medicine are big subjects. The horses have opened a door for us to look through because they simply want us to know they are affected more than we comprehend. They are asking us to take a different look at our practices, a look from the horse's point of view. It is interesting to note that Malt, himself, had been given only a few immunizations in his life.

Malt showed about his "soft-eyed" human. Having soft eyes means learning to work with a horse's inner systems, in this case the immune system. A strong immune system allows the horse to stay in balance and supports his innate ability to repair himself. The horses see what humans call diseases as part of the dance with the unseen beings.

The development of chemicals and drugs to control diseases is a well-accepted part of the human approach to maintaining horses' health. In addition, the horses are also showing us that humans have emotional and fear components in their attack on disease. This powerful three-fold push—chemicals, emotions and fear—can force a horse's delicate inner systems out of balance.

I want to be VERY CLEAR that I am not implying or saying, "Don't vaccinate." Malt was showing us that vaccines have adverse effects on horses, and we can use that information to decide what to do. Each of us gets to take a look from the horses' point of view. That is all the horses are asking.

Their point of view is different from our human point of view. Their view of life is simpler. Horses are asking us to take a simpler look at how we manage them. They are asking us to see that horses have great inner power to repair themselves when their overall bodily systems are in balance.

Horses are also asking us to look at how our fear and emotions affect how we manage them. With what the horses have shown me, I have learned to look at my emotions and fear. I see how they get in the way. It is not a straight line and over many years my point of view is changing. I am learning that simpler is better. I am accepting death as a part of life. People and horses die in my life, and life goes on.

I've learned I can detach from my emotions. It doesn't mean I don't care or don't get upset. The upsets, however, are not as long or deep as they used to be. A shorter period of grief is not an indication of a lesser degree of love.

It feels scary to realize I can't control everything, yet it is great letting go of control and letting things be. The horses have taught me that little steps of learning create huge realizations.

What you, the reader, do with the information presented by the horses is up to you. Our choices create how we live our lives. I've learned life is a daily unfolding. When I surrender and allow, rather than control, my days are filled with amazing adventures. As hard as this chapter was to do, I would not have missed it for anything. Our horses are truly wonderful.

Journey's End

April 16, 2007, evening

When Malt finished giving me the information for the chapter on vaccinations last summer, I stopped writing. I now know why. It wasn't time to write the ending piece because it wasn't ready.

Malt had one more gift to give. I found him down in the pasture with colic. I called his owner, Cheryl, from my cell phone, and asked her to come down. We decided I would go to the barn and prepare a stall, while Cheryl led Malt up to the barn.

I walked into the barn and heard a loud groan. I quickly walked down the aisle, and in the last stall found a mare, Freckles, trying to deliver her foal. The foal, a beautiful filly, was jammed between her dam's hindquarters and the center beam of the stall. Her hind legs were still inside Freckles, and she was still encased in the amniotic sac. Normally, this sac breaks during birth, but it had not, and the foal was suffocating. I immediately cut the sac from around her nostrils and head, and gently pulled her so her hindquarters and legs were free. The filly started to wiggle and move her legs—nice healthy movements. I quietly left the stall, letting the mare and filly alone.

We called the vet and he came quickly. I stood at Malt's head while Richard examined him. Malt showed me he was dying. I didn't want to believe it. He and I were going to be riding partners this summer. We had a bond, and I was finally going to ride again.

The diagnosis was a twist in Malt's large colon. Surgery was not an option. Malt was not ready to go just yet. He told me not to be sad. His job was done; experiencing West Nile virus allowed him the ability to give us the information on vaccines. This is what he came to do, and now he was free to go. I opened my heart and showed him I was fine and the door was wide open.

April 17, 2007, mid-morning

Malt made it clear he was ready to go. I called Richard to come, and then made the arrangements for Malt's body to be buried. Malt was down, but when he heard Richard's truck, he got up. I put Malt's halter on and *he led me* out the stall door. We had a peaceful last half-hour. Malt ate some grass, and we walked over to the gate of the gelding's pasture so he could whinny a good bye. That done, he was ready.

One life arriving, another one leaving. The movement and rhythm of horses. So simple. The filly's name is Malted Riki, after Malt, a great horse, and Richard, a great vet.

Life is movement. Just like Mimi said.

About the Author

Sandy Lagno grew up in the beautiful horse country of Dutchess County, New York. At the age of 5, her Dad bought Sandy a horse and she became a life-long student of horses. Joining the United States Pony Club at age 12, Sandy achieved her B Rating in 1965, demonstrating horsemanship knowledge and proficiency, and her leadership ability, at the national level. Deborah Dows, who founded Southlands in Rhinebeck, New York, and was trained at the Spanish Riding School, soon became Sandy's instructor and mentor. Sandy received classical training in riding, barn management, and horse care from this stern taskmaster.

Photo by "Duffy" (Edith) Schade, 1964, Litchfield, CT

In 1981, Sandy was accepted into the Head Instructor Training program at the Cheff Therapeutic Riding Center in Augusta, Michigan. After graduating, she stayed on as a therapeutic riding instructor for children and adults with all types of disabilities.

Over the years, Sandy has been assistant manager of large horse barns, as well as having shown in both English and western equitation classes. She has trained and exercised field hunters, fox hunted, evented, and exercised cutting and endurance horses. Sandy enjoyed filling much of her time instructing children, adult beginners and riders with fear issues. She has studied with professionals like George Morris, Locke Richards, Barbara Schulte, Linda Tellington-Jones and Richard Thompson. Now a quiet trail ride suits her fine.

In 1997, Sandy started her inter-species translation work. Since then, she has worked with horses and their owners, farriers, veterinarians and trainers, translating what horses show her. Sandy is helping to create a better understanding between horses and humans, and therefore, helping people make better choices in caring for their horses.